P9-DTX-778

Pelican Books A640

Discrimination and Popular Culture

Denys Thompson read Classics and English at
Cambridge. He taught English at Hitchin
Grammar School and at Gresham's School,
Holt, became a temporary civil servant, and
then Headmaster of the Yeovil School until
1962. He has done a good deal of lecturing,
especially overseas, on the teaching of
English. Now engaged in writing, advising,
and editing, he recently took the initiative in
the starting of the National Association
for the Teaching of English. He is an author
(often with Raymond O'Malley) and
editor of books for schools, ranging from
an anthology for primary schools to *Science
in Perspective*, and he assisted F. R. Leavis
with *Culture and Environment*. He has
been editor for twenty-five years of the
quarterly *The Use of English* and of its
predecessor *English in Schools*.

Denys Thompson is married and has
a son and a daughter. He enjoys reading,
gardening, travel, and walking in Dorset.

Discrimination and Popular Culture

Edited by Denys Thompson

Penguin Books

BALTIMORE · MARYLAND

P
90
.T45

Penguin Books Ltd, Harmondsworth,
Middlesex, England
Penguin Books Inc., 3300 Clipper Mill Road,
Baltimore 11, Md, U.S.A.
Penguin Books Pty Ltd, Ringwood,
Victoria, Australia

First published by Penguin Books 1964

Copyright © Penguin Books, 1964

Made and printed in Great Britain by
C. Nicholls & Company Ltd

Set in Intertype Times

Contents

Foreword

In October 1960 the National Union of Teachers held a Conference with the title 'Popular Culture and Personal Responsibility'. The aim was 'to examine the impact of mass communications on present-day moral and cultural standards'. It was attended by large numbers 'of those engaged in education together with parents, those concerned with the welfare of children and young people, and people involved in the mass media themselves'.

Since then the NUT has been exploring ways of helping young people, teachers, youth leaders, and parents to realize the need for discrimination in accepting the offerings of the mass media. The present book is intended to be a step towards the positive use for good of the mass media. It is thus a direct outcome of the 1960 Conference, but not the only one – there are other means whereby the NUT is following up the suggestions then made.

The Editor's thanks are due to Fred Jarvis (NUT), Dieter Pevsner (Penguin Books), David Holbrook, Brian Jackson, and especially Raymond O'Malley for their advice at various stages.

D.T.

1   Introduction

DENYS THOMPSON

Applied science has enormously increased the world's population. The extra people live mainly in large units that tend more and more to resemble each other. They have to be reached by their governments and by all the agencies that wish to impart news, opinions, and announcements of goods and services for sale. The town crier, the notice in the church porch, and the back-street printer have been replaced by the means – radio, popular press, and advertising – that technology has made possible. The next gifts of applied science to very large numbers of people were more leisure, more energy to enjoy it, and a much greater spending power. And as a result home-made amusements, live performances, and inexpensive hobbies are now supplanted by a large and well-organized entertainment industry that reaches deeply into our homes and pockets. Much that used to be supplied locally is now centrally provided by newspapers, publicity, radio, film, records, magazines, and the mass-production of things used and enjoyed in the home.

The reformers of the nineteenth century nobly hoped that the workers, once freed from the prison of illiteracy and long hours, would give themselves a liberal education and feed on the same intellectual delights as the reformers themselves. Their disappointed hopes may have been pitched too high: today our expectations of popular culture seem altogether too low. The hypothesis of this book is that the shortcomings of popular culture are with us because the mass media just listed have become the expression and mouthpiece of a particular type of civilization. One, that is, in which our productive powers have acquired a life of their own and run away with us. The drift can certainly be checked and society acquire a sense of direction, but up to the present changes seem to have been too swift for us fully to control them or successfully adapt ourselves to them. The mass media affect our lives closely at many points, perhaps more intimately than we are aware of. This book is an attempt by its authors to throw light upon this influence.

The pervasiveness of the media is made possible by mass-production, which gives us cheap and efficient printed matter and receiving-sets. The implications of mass-production are worth considering. It needs a great deal of capital. In oil refining, for instance, the cost of the plant per person employed is about £12,500; in chemicals it may reach £30,000. Thus idle plant can be ruinous; as far as possible it must be worked all day and every day. The same applies to the means of reaching people. Newspapers must circulate, not only to gain advertising, but to ensure that the capital locked up in forests and pulp-making shows a return. A Sunday paper may be started, not to meet a demand, but because it will occupy presses that would otherwise be unprofitably still. Again, the specialized machinery for producing paper-backs is so costly that it must be kept moving; and new techniques for printing text-books in colour involve so expensive a setting-up that 'it is not worth printing fewer than 100,000 or even 250,000 copies'. If we turn to the film industry, we find that an average film costs £150,000 in the two months it takes to make, and an exceptional one may need £3,000,000.

Much of what applies to the mass-production of goods is true also of the mass media. The people who handle the large capital invested are under an obligation to see that it shows a profit, so the media, or the plant which produces them, must be employed for as many hours of the twenty-four as possible. We might be better off if newspapers were smaller, paper-backs fewer, and television much reduced in quantity. But even if the controllers agreed, they could not do much about it; they are there to keep the machinery going. Quantity becomes more important than quality, and poor quality is concealed by dazzlingly efficient presentation.

Other features of mass-production are also found in the mass media. What is presented must be 'safe', unprovocative and

10

generally acceptable. Individual preferences are ignored, because mass-production pays best when millions of copies of a few designs are turned out, rather than fewer copies of more designs. Thus mass communications 'exercise a constant pressure upon their users to invoke similar responses from the largest numbers of people.' At present the 'similar responses' tend to be at a low level, for the controllers generally aim at the lowest common factors to be found in the audience. Again, the sub-division of work that characterizes mass-production is found also in films, radio, and pop music. In the latter for example we are told that 'the sole contribution of the composer is his ability to whistle a little tune which he is incapable of writing on paper. Then the skilled services of the arranger come into play ...'. Responsibility is divided till it ceases to exist.

Though the controllers of the media claim 'freedom' for their activities, they seem very much to be prisoners of the conditions we have described. As long as they aim merely at big audiences, so long will their behaviour be predictable. While the market is the test of what shall be disseminated, the controllers appear to be the tools of impersonal forces, and in their subservience they are bound to provide us with worse fare than we deserve or the media are capable of. Their apology for their present practice is that they 'give the public what it wants', and they interpret the acquiescence of the public as positive approval. But without good reason. Very few indeed of the readers of popular newspapers, for example, would applaud the ruthless and inhuman methods of the reporters who intrude on grief, extract 'reactions' from distressed people, betray confidences. These things are done because the controllers think they ought to be done. Most of us again may have a streak of the ghoul within us, which we usually subordinate to better impulses. But in the conditions imposed on them editors and reporters see all their readers as ghouls if there are corpses available. The controllers in sum have no vital contact with their audience; they are ignorant of its composition and history; they cannot see people for TAM ratings and ABC figures.

11

According to the controllers, the masses do not want to learn; they want only to be entertained. But (as the late J. Trenaman commented after some years' work on television) there is no research or evidence to support such a view, whereas there is evidence to the contrary. If the controllers are right, then people like being sold rubbish and enjoy being deceived by advertising. Both selling rubbish and deception are widespread, according to the 'Molony' Report, but they continue because the consumer accepts his disappointment philosophically or puts it down to his own misjudgement. Something of the kind happens with the other mass media; 'giving the public what it wants' turns out to mean disposing of goods or entertainment that will vaguely satisfy a large number of people, without prompting active interest or approval. As Lord Hailsham said of television:

The TAM rating can be, I think sometimes is, a melancholy record of third and fourth preferences – the maximum number of viewers who can be induced not to turn off, the highest common factor of endurance without enthusiasm.

Even if the controllers were able to establish in a particular case that there was a genuine preference for what they supply, they would almost certainly be found to have created the taste for it. For what sells most is not necessarily the best product or the best value for money; it is more likely to be the most efficiently publicized and pushed. As Mr Farr so convincingly shows, the sales of a product are by no means an indication of what the consumer wants. The overriding concern of the controllers is profit, and they naturally manipulate the public taste if they can. The extent of their power can be over-estimated – there is not enough evidence, for one rarely comes across so revealing a statement as that made by H. Ratcliffe, of the Musicians' Union. Discussing popular music and records, he said:

Any music publisher can tell you six months ahead which tune is going to be popular. The public does not make a tune popular. Subject to certain exceptions, some flukes here and there, we know in advance what is going to be popular six months ahead, and the publishing business makes sure a tune it wants to be popular is popular, by spending enough money to make it popular.

Characteristically the controllers, wielding power without true responsibility over audiences they never meet, despise them. Only contempt can account for the quality of some of the offerings. One can sense it in many an advertisement and commercial, and perhaps in this reported quotation from Cecil King, Chairman of Daily Mirror Newspapers, Ltd: 'In point of fact it is only the people who conduct newspapers and similar organizations who have any idea quite how indifferent, quite how stupid, quite how uninterested in education of any kind the great bulk of the British public are.' A different point of view is put by Arnold Wesker:

It is the age of the big insult – trivia pays larger dividends, therefore trivia must be what is wanted. Is this a deliberate policy to keep the nation cretinized by trivialities or does it stem from a profound belief that the people of this country are cretins from the start?

Owing to their cynicism and ignorance of the variety and resources of their audiences, the controllers are sometimes astoundingly inept in deciding and arranging what shall be consumed – despite all the slickness of presentation. And the 'freedom' they talk about is one-sided. There can be no freedom for viewer or reader without choice; and people can make a real choice only if they have a more than superficial acquaintance with the possibilities. This knowledge of the range of things to choose from is just what the controllers in general do not find it possible to supply. The hunt for mass audiences, needed to attract advertising or pay for it, causes the controllers to narrow the field of taste in which people can discriminate; 'they will be kept unaware of what lies beyond the average of experience.'

We exist as a nation to produce more goods. That is the answer one would get from a spokesman for any political party. Increased production is the common cry, with small mention of the nature and quality and destination of what is to be produced. It seems odd to anyone who thinks back a generation

13

or so. The need then was to produce more so that no one should go without; easier times were just round the corner. We have rounded the corner and – with some exceptions – no one need go without in a welfare state. But we are still incited to produce more, to keep up with the neighbours at home or abroad. Not yet is the worker allowed to enjoy the fruit of his labour in leisure. Most workers now have more than their grandfathers would have thought enough. The basic needs are fulfilled, but fresh ones are constantly being created by advertising; and leisure is now to be regarded, under the same pressure, as an opportunity to spend on advertised goods and services. One example of the fresh needs is the extension of one sex's habits to the other. The effort has been made to make drinking in pubs respectable for girls and women, while for men it is no longer effeminate to use scent, provided it is sold as after-shave lotion.

Some of the best comments on the process are made by Professor J. K. Galbraith. Observing that 'one cannot defend production as satisfying wants if that production creates the wants', he continues:

Were it so that a man on arising each morning was assailed by demons which instilled in him a passion sometimes for silk shirts, sometimes for kitchenware, sometimes for chamber-pots, and sometimes for orange squash, there would be every reason to applaud the effort to find the goods, however odd, that quenched this flame. But should it be that his passion was the result of his first having cultivated the demons, and should it be also that his effort to allay it stirred the demons to even greater and greater effort, there would be question as to how rational was his solution .... He might wonder if the solution lay with more goods or fewer demons.... Production only fills a void that it has itself created.

The charge against advertising that it distorts a nation's economy was first made a good many years ago, and Professor Galbraith enlarges it with a wealth of example, stressing especially private affluence with public poverty. Such opinions may be very important, but they do not get much of a hearing in press and radio, for

With the exception of the BBC the mass media are part of this process – production for its own sake. Advertising, broadcasting, and the Press make the consumer goods seem indispensable for happiness. Films and magazines work closely with them to glorify the consuming life. Records tax the leisure that might otherwise pay too small a tribute, and a host of goods of indifferent design and quality multiply the occasions for spending and display.

It may be said that there is nothing very dreadful in all this, though the creation of artificial wants to be satisfied by consumer goods is hardly a satisfactory aim for a society. The controllers supply entertainment which more or less contents a good many people, and why should anyone worry? But of course there is very little 'pure' entertainment. The individual's capacity for thought and feeling is being strengthened or weakened all the time by what he sees and hears, and his views (about the social order, for instance) may derive entirely from entertainment. 'Entertainment' is much of it a form of propaganda for things as they are, relentlessly pressing us to be good conformers and avid consumers. Again, however good entertainment may be, it must at present be an occasion for spending and a means of profit to somebody. This condition excludes all sorts of civilized diversions.

Members of the 1960 Conference felt that there was more to it than entertainment. The most noticeable thread running through the proceedings was the express hostility of teachers towards the way in which the mass media are used at present. For example: 'There is bound to be a very sharp conflict between the task of education and the role of the media, which are still closely linked to securing profit and to the advertising industry' (Stuart Hall). The feeling was so strong that the word 'media' was evidently felt to be a misnomer; they were not just vehicles for transmitting news and views and entertainment – they provided the views, filtered the news, and devised a special kind of entertainment. As Abrams demonstrates so clearly, those who operate the channels decide what shall flow through them. They have created the taste, often entirely new in scale and often in kind, for what they supply to their public. All the same, it is pointless to isolate the mass media in the

15

dock; rather should we look critically at the civilization in which the offerings of the entertainment industry are necessary and acceptable.

'The selves we are are to a great extent the product of our social contacts.' It may be that these social contacts are being replaced by the mass media; what they supply for us to read and hear and see may influence us decisively. Our national culture is being replaced by a synthetic substance that exists only in the media. For instance, no one outside an agency ever talks like an advertisement; and the attitudes of the popular press are rarely a crystallization of what any of their readers feel, just as the language in which the news is conveyed is a special one never spoken in real life. The 'midatlantic' speech of entertainers and others exists at present only on radio and television, though doubtless it will soon spread thence. Television in particular is seen by some observers to be the agent of moral and aesthetic education, supplying a continuous stream of attitude-forming information under the label of entertainment, replacing the teaching of church and family and school. So that:

> Faced with this kind of pressure the responsibility of the teacher becomes very great. Matched against the glib facility of a radio commentator supported by all the gimmicks and aids to presentation, the classroom teacher is gravely hampered in an age in which the titillation of public fancy has become a matter of professional expertise. His influence on adolescent minds has to be weighed against that of ephemeral stars of film or T.V. screen. The easy success of popular entertainers is in great contrast to the sustained effort needed to achieve anything worth while in other spheres – and especially in the school.

Year Book of Education 1960

If the criticisms, on educational grounds, of the industry are valid, teachers are wasting their time. Children are taught to read – up to a point; they leave school with the ability to skim the surface of advertisements and newspapers and magazines. Nowadays this is not enough; children need not only to be given a tool, but taught how to use it. Teachers are not to blame if their pupils are less than half-educated, for schools are still organized to prepare entrants to industry instead of providing education for life.

There are of course many schools that teach their pupils how to understand the language of advertising, to read between the lines of the Press, to discriminate between films, to 'go shopping' on T.V., and to see the difference between good and bad design in town and country. All schools should give some instruction of this kind. As it is, school-leavers are too often a ready prey for the mass media, and everything acquired at school in the way of aesthetic and moral training is contradicted and attacked by the entertainment industry. As the Director of Education for Derbyshire remarked, 'the functions which the community has entrusted [to teachers] are too often inhibited, frustrated, or completely defeated because those they care for succumb to the attraction of other doctrines and values'. Young people are supplied with a well-packaged, superficially attractive but fake culture, thought up by the entertainers, who exploit any elements of genuinely popular culture that may survive.

This is not speculation. The attitudes encouraged by an advertisement-fed Press, the effect of films on children, the impact of television (so lucidly analysed in Dr Himmelweit's book) – about these and much else there is plenty of observation and research on record.

The mass media miss their opportunities of being a healthy force in the nation's life, because they are subservient to advertising or fit in too readily with the general drift of the times. When we come to action, it looks as if (at least so far as the young are concerned) the principle whereby people are protected from themselves as well as from plain exploitation will have to be extended. The nineteenth century maimed and enslaved the worker's body; perhaps in the twentieth it is his mind that is maintained in servile contentment. Action based on this view is bound to be met with the criticism that it is paternalist, just as the Factory Acts were opposed for sapping the workers' independence. Such objections cannot be made to restrictions on the use of dangerous drugs, because drugs belong to the field of science. Here everything is measurable and

17

predictable, and the scientist is respected. Critics of the mass media are unlikely to carry such weight, though their views may be as valid as those of the scientists, and the things they criticize as dangerous as drugs. 'I know what I like' will no more help the man in the street to choose his entertainment than it will enable him to cope with the noises of detergent advertising. Experts are needed in the sphere of 'cultural' health as much as they are for bodily health – to ensure that there is a range over which real choice can be exercised, that conformity of any kind is not imposed, and that our distinctive national culture is kept alive and accessible. There need be no paternalism, any more than there is paternalism in the attitude of the teacher, concerned to do his best for those for whom he is responsible, but not to coerce or bully them. It is to the educator that we must look for part of the answer to problems of the mass media. Already education can probably claim some credit for the disrepute of advertising and the success of the Consumers' Associations.

This is more than a pious hope. Education is a point at which the ideas and efforts of men and women of goodwill can be focused. It can be effective, because in this country as in no other it is independent of governmental and political and commercial pressures and is free to develop a purpose and philosophy of its own.

In passing, there is one argument in favour of letting things take their course that must be met. Sometimes it is suggested that in the Middle Ages people were much more standardized in a church-dominated society than they are today. They had little choice; they had small hope of changing their station; they were in some ways stereotyped. But they were free from the unremitting pressure of advertising, and the influences that did affect them were of a different order from those of today. The difference was summed up in his Granada Lecture by Sir Eric Ashby:

> Every Sunday the peasant at the Mass was (as it were) irrigated from the main stream of European society. The benefits to him were not only spiritual. His eyes rested on lovely craftsmanship. He heard Palestrina's music. He learnt unconsciously something of

the standards of art and music and oratory which were the pride of Europe.

However, we should not expect too much of education in the short run. Other action should be taken, especially to reduce the influence of advertising. We need not take too seriously the adman's claims about the immediate power of advertising, but we ought to be concerned about its long-term, agenda-making effects. Those who control the mass media must be made fully responsible to the society on which they live. It should, for example, be impossible for a leading figure in advertising to claim that 'commercial television is first and foremost an advertising medium and only secondarily and in-cidentally a public service.' Things are out of control when with one hand we spend £1,000m a year on education, includ-ing all the physical facilities, and with the other give the adver-tisers £500m a year for what is largely anti-education. Anti, both because of the very special way of life, in which consump-tion is the whole duty of man, heralded by advertising, and because the media used by advertising tend to become ancil-lary to it. Society must remove the pressure of advertising on television and the newspapers, and not leave it to the schools to retrieve the damage.

Education has a double answer to the mass media as they are used at present, if two requisites can be satisfied. The first is freedom for the teacher to get on with the job as he or she thinks best, and that condition is very largely secured already. The teacher in England has probably more scope than his coun-terpart in any part of the world. The second is a supply of teach-ers informed about mass communications and with some idea of how to use them. Some training colleges are doing excellent work in this direction.

Education can deal directly with the media in school, as many schools have been doing for thirty years. The analysis of advertisements, study of the Press (starting with elementary comparison of two newspapers), the teaching of discrimination in films, T.V., music, and design – all these have been profit-ably carried out, and at various levels. Raymond Williams

19

enlarges on these approaches in his *Communications*, and adds:

The work ... is particularly important in adolescence: in the leaving years especially, for it is then that the conflict between the values of school and the values of the adult world is most obvious. There is no need, however, for the work to be confined to schools. It should be a central part of the new liberal studies courses in technical colleges, and of apprentice courses. It should form a main part of informal work in the youth service, and it should be a normal subject ... in adult education.

Once again, too much should not be demanded of education; perhaps too much is asked already. The individual must learn to discriminate if he is to grapple with the approaches of the mass media, but the schools can give no more than a start; the mature judgement and the range of information that are needed are acquired in adulthood. The start, however, may be all-important – teachers can be sure that the seeds they sow will bear fruit. At present, as we have seen, there is not enough choosing; we tend somewhat passively to accept what is thrust upon us. The better education becomes, the less passivity and acquiescence there will be. Schools can impart an awareness of the possibilities and an inclination to go shopping among the media, using them positively, rather than being used by them. Though not all teachers are willing and equipped to give their pupils lessons in discrimination, schools can still pursue one central purpose, and many of them do, supremely well. That is, to bring their pupils into as much contact as possible with the first-rate in art, literature, and music, all widely conceived.

The aim is to provide children with standards (starting with the small details of everyday life) against which the offerings of the mass media will appear cut down to size. With some children this may just be a pious hope, but not with all; many teachers know that what they offer sticks. It means supplying the very best in buildings and equipment; in all sorts of experience in extra-curricular goings-on; in ethics and in manners, so relevant in a dense population. All this presupposes the best teachers and the best training for them, but it is not wishful

thinking, for many schools already do all that one could require of them. At the 1960 Conference J. L. Longland vividly
contrasted the intelligence, interests, and activities of children
at school with the dullness of routine jobs and the offerings of
mass communications, which 'corrupt good manners [and] continuously under-employ faculties ... Too often the school
seems to sit in the middle of an adult and workaday world like
an oasis in a wide desert.'

The mass media then are a product of the technology to
which we owe, perhaps our lives, almost certainly our health,
and much that makes life worth living. Except for the BBC,
they are commercial enterprises that need to show a profit.
They therefore go all out for the highest circulation figures,
and this seems to ensure that the bulk of their output is of poor
quality. Our rich national culture is replaced by a synthetic
affair, which glamorizes a consumption-for-its-own-sake civilization. A tolerant public acquiesces in this.

The importance of the mass media is that they fill much of
people's leisure, and with shorter hours and less absorbing
work leisure is almost the whole of life. It is in leisure, not in
work, that most people nowadays really live and find themselves. More and more what we do with our leisure decides the
quality of our living. If this is correct, the mass media matter a
great deal; they may well be altering the aims and character of
the nation. They certainly seem to be a main formative influence on young people.

The mass media are here to stay, and whether we use them
to enrich our lives or are used by them as circulation-fodder is
the test of our civilization. They could encourage the interests
and activities wherein men and women would meet the challenge that work now fails to offer – the challenge to try out
their physical and mental strength. They could keep to the
fore matters of public concern – art, education, aid to needy
countries, the regeneration of towns – that are neglected when
attention is attracted elsewhere. They could do something to
put people in touch with the cultural heritage that is at present
fenced off from them. If we are to have a genuine popular culture with its roots in society, the mass media must continue

21

where education at its best leaves off. No great improvement can be expected till more and better education makes its impact and the media are met by a consciously discriminating public. The surest advance in the end could come from an education that nourishes the imagination, trains the emotions and strengthens the ability to choose.

*

BOOKS

SIR ERIC ASHBY, 'Dons or Crooners' in *Communication in the Modern World* (Granada T.V.)

J. K. GALBRAITH, *The Affluent Society* (Penguin Books)

BRIAN GROOMBRIDGE, *A Study Outline* (National Union of Teachers) Discussion points and questions on the mass media.

DANIEL JENKINS, *Equality and Excellence* (SCM Press)

RAYMOND WILLIAMS, *Communications* (Penguin Books) *Verbatim Report* of the Conference on Popular Culture and Personal Responsibility (National Union of Teachers). *Year Book of Education 1960*: (Evans Bros.) Communication Media and the School.

2   Advertising

FRANK WHITEHEAD

Advertising slogans can range all the way from the trite ('Beer, it's lovely') through the vulgarly inane ('You'll look a little lovelier each day with Fabulous Pink Camay') to the idiotically bizarre ('I dreamed I made sweet music in my Maidenform bra'). For the advertising executive there is only one criterion to be applied to all of them: Will they induce people to buy more of the article in question, more Brand A, more beer, more soap, more brassières? Any effect that advertising has upon our culture or values or language is thus unintended and (from the copywriter's point of view) strictly irrelevant – but that doesn't make the influence any less potent or less far-reaching. Indeed if culture is 'the whole way of life of a community' there is a case for saying that the cultural kingpin of twentieth-century Britain is the advertising industry. Certainly no one today can escape continual assault by advertisements in one form or another. (Can *you* remember a day this year when no advertiser's message reached you – not even a hoarding, a shop-window display, a phrase on a cereal packet?) And in 1961 expenditure on all forms of advertising in the United Kingdom reached a record total of £470 millions – an amount which compares interestingly with a net expenditure of £418 millions in the same year on all primary and secondary schools in England and Wales.

These vast sums are spent by business firms in the expectation of specific economic advantages, and the exponents of advertising (usually employees of advertising agencies) who are so assiduous in writing letters to the Press usually base their defence on the claim that a modern industrial economy 'cannot exist without advertising'. The economic case for advertising must be examined later. The main concern of this essay is

23

with its unplanned yet pervasive influence upon the quality of our thinking and feeling, and upon the goals towards which we strive both in our individual lives and in the network of social relationships which make up our civilization. There are two main questions to be asked here. First, what kinds of emotional appeal do advertisers find it profitable to play upon, and what is the effect on our sensibilities of the copywriter's persistent harping upon these feelings? Second, in what ways does financial dependence upon advertisements affect the quality, content, and availability of the media (newspapers, magazines, television, and radio programmes) through which advertising is disseminated?

Before we consider these issues, however, it must be made clear that there is a great deal of advertising which we can safely ignore because it confines itself, unexceptionably, to providing information about goods and services for sale. Broadly speaking, the classified advertisements, in small print, in a newspaper fall under this heading; as do the majority of advertisements in trade and technical journals which are directed at other manufacturers or traders; together with a certain number of the display advertisements for local shopkeepers which appear in local daily or weekly papers. At the opposite pole are almost all television commercials and most of the display advertisements in national daily and Sunday papers and large-circulation magazines – a very high proportion, in fact, of all the nation-wide advertising which is addressed to the ordinary purchaser or final consumer. These advertisements contain a minimum of informational content and set out primarily to work upon our feelings and half-conscious attitudes by non-rational suggestion. This distinction between 'informational advertising' and 'advertising by psychological manipulation' is admittedly a rough and ready one, and there are many dubious cases in the borderland between the two. Thus 'Asphalting contractor: drives and paths re-surfaced from 10s. square yard; phone — ' falls clearly enough in the one category; while 'It's smart to drink Port' belongs unmistakably to the other. We might find it harder to agree on a classification for the single-line advertisement which appeared in the *New Statesman*'s Personal Column for many years: 'French taught by Parisienne; Results guaranteed'.

STRATEGIES OF PERSUASION

To persuade people to a course of action by reasoned argument would seem to be a perfectly legitimate procedure for the propagandist, whether political or commercial. The advertising 'profession' has long been of the opinion, however, that human beings in the mass are more malleable if you address your appeal not to their intelligence, but to their private fears, anxieties, prejudices, and day-dreams. The strategy employed has been aptly characterized by Aldous Huxley:

Find some common desire, some widespread unconscious fear or anxiety; think out some way to relate this wish or fear to the product you have to sell; then, build a bridge of verbal or pictorial symbols over which your customer can pass from fact to compensatory dream, and from the dream to the illusion that your product, when purchased, will make the dream come true.

The method can be studied at its crudest in the picture-strips which tell the predictable story of the housewife whose marriage was nearly wrecked because she failed to drink the right brand of night-time beverage or the courier who nearly missed promotion because he had omitted to protect himself against B.O. by using one particular brand of toilet soap.

Reliance upon such appeals (what Thorstein Veblen called 'a trading on the range of human infirmities') tends to breed a peculiarly distasteful form of contempt for human nature. The attitude can be studied in these off-the-cuff observations from the Vice-President of one of the world's largest advertising agencies (quoted by Martin Mayer in *Madison Avenue, U.S.A.*):

People are very much alike the world over. You try to take something away from them, they resist. They all want some security. They're all a little lazy. And there isn't a housewife anywhere who doesn't want to look presentable – or wants to hear the truth about how she really looks.

25

The same outlook was given more guarded expression in an advertisement for a leading British advertising agency which appeared in a quality daily newspaper in 1960:

PEOPLE ARE ONLY HUMAN

Let's keep them that way. Let's resist any suggestion that they are statistics or cardboard cut-outs or unseen unknowns. People are people.

Oh yes, men are sometimes the smiling, extrovert athletes who look out on us from hoardings and cathode screens. But mostly, remember, men are home lovers and gardeners; they visit their parents and they play with their children; they sing sentimental songs in the pub, and they know the taste of fear.

Oh yes, women are sometimes the smiling, porcelain figures who look out on us from beside the athletes. But mostly, remember, women are mothers and housewives; they visit the shops and they play with their children; they sing sentimental songs at the sink, and they know the taste of tears.

These are the people (there are no others!) we must needs reach with our products, our services, our ideas.

There's nothing unreal or unfathomable about people. They're only human.

This is in itself an intriguing example of the copywriter's craft; it leads off with an incontrovertible platitude (carefully designed to suggest a community of fellow-feeling between writer and reader), and then keeps our attention with a button-holing insistence thinly overlaid by a beguilingly near-conversational intimacy of tone. Flattery is an indispensable weapon in the persuader's armoury, so a little uplift is thrown in for good measure; but the most perfunctory of pseudo-poetic echoes ('know the taste of fear', 'know the taste of tears', 'must needs') are evidently all you need in this line, even for an intellectual *élite* (in this case the *Guardian* readership). There must be a certain defensiveness of stance behind the desire to dissociate *this* agency from the irritated disbelief aroused by the glossy stereotypes who figure in T.V. commercials; but the allegedly more 'real' alternative is presented with a revealingly cynical condescension. One might know that it would be *sentimental* songs which 'they' sing in pubs and at sinks. And the keynote of the whole ethos is surely contained in the words 'nothing unfathomable'; this is the aspect of our common humanity which the adman will do his utmost to perpetuate.

In recent years the advertising world has turned increasingly to the twin techniques of market research and motivational research, in order to make more efficient its empirically-gained knowledge of how best to work upon human frailty. Market research uses sampling methods borrowed from sociology in order to find out who buys a particular article and its rival brands, and then to classify the purchasers or potential purchasers in terms of age, sex, locality, income-level, and social status; the advertising agency can then select the appeal judged most appropriate for members of this social grouping, and place its advertisements in the media which are most likely to reach them. Motivational research is linked in many people's minds with the name of its most aggressive propagandist, the American Dr Ernest Dichter; it uses a somewhat dubious version of depth psychology to establish, by a paraphernalia of 'depth interviews', psychodrama, and projective tests, the unconscious significance which any commodity has for its purchasers. Thus Unilever's agency Lintas a few years ago 'wrung from forty women the surprising information that soap is subconsciously viewed as something potentially harmful: the ideal soap is not the one that does most good but the one that does least harm'; this provided the rationale for an advertising campaign in which Astral cream soap was claimed to be 'less drying' to the skin and 'baby mild'. Similarly the Maidenform Bra series of advertisements ('I Dreamed I Stopped Traffic in my Maidenform Bra') in which a young woman walked about in her brassière among normally dressed people were said to be justified because of the exhibitionist tendency in all of us which makes us wish to appear naked or scantily dressed in a crowd.

In spite of these pseudo-scientific refinements the main types of appeal in use today remain very much the same as those which were anatomized by F. R. Leavis and Denys Thompson in *Culture and Environment* (1933). There is still much exploitation of fear in various forms – fear of losing one's job, fear of failure in courtship or marriage or parenthood, fear of what the neighbours will think if the clothes on your washing-line are only white and not 'dazzling-white' or of what the shopkeeper must think when you ask for 'inferior toilet-paper'. The fear of social inferiority is the theme of a recent series of advertisements for one of the 'Big Five' banks, in which a young woman realizes that she is getting less courteous attention in a department store than the other customers because she pays cash for her purchases instead of paying by cheque. (An unlikely situation, one would have thought, in real life, but perhaps these advertisements may yet succeed in bringing it about.) Carrying the same implication that the all-important issue is not what you are but what other people think of you, are the numerous advertisements which sell us clothes, furniture, motor-cars, refrigerators as status-symbols – an opportunity for conspicuous expenditure which will impress the Joneses next door as evidence of our opulence and refinement. (Similarly, State Express 555 is claimed to be 'the cigarette that goes with success', while Churchman's No. 1 is said to be appreciated by 'men of judgement', a characteristic which it shares with several brands of whisky.) Such claims for exclusiveness are often of course addled from the start, since the advertisements are in reality directed not at a minority but at the self-deluding majority. However, the advertiser can always try the alternative approach of tapping our innate impulse towards unthinking conformity ('millions' smoke this cigarette, 'everyone' enjoys this ice-cream); we are all inclined to feel safer if we know we are only doing what other people do, and it's no concern of the adman if, in thus eroding a little more of our belief in the importance of individual judgement, he carries us a step farther along the road towards 'other-directed' living (David Riesman's phrase) as opposed to the 'inner-directed' morality which has been the mainspring for all the major cultural achievements of Western civilization.

Another well-tried appeal still much in vogue is that which trades upon our superstitious faith in 'scientific' authority. In advertisements for toothpaste, disinfectants, patent medicines, beauty preparations, and the like, a young man in a white coat (it may not be explicitly stated that he is a doctor or research scientist) dispenses polysyllabic mumbo-jumbo which is all the more impressive because we don't in the least understand it. Recently this exploitation of hypochondria has been extended to our pets, so that we are exhorted nowadays to make sure that our budgerigar doesn't go short on vitamins, and that our cat gets its full quota of minerals and marrowbone jelly. Working in a similar way in a different field is the claim that 'No other *soap-filled* pad works like a Trojan because now it contains a Foam-Booster'. We might reasonably ask whether foam is either necessary or helpful to the cleaning-action of wire wool, since consumer reports have revealed that some synthetic detergents can work perfectly well with little or no foam, and that manufacturers add a foaming agent (usually alkylolamide) not to improve the efficiency of their product but to induce a feeling of confidence in housewives who associate plentiful lather, in soap, with cleaning power. The copywriter, however, is relying upon the loaded word ('Foam-Booster') to head us off from making any such inquiry. If we refuse to be lulled (or battered) into acquiescence we usually find that any statement that may be wrapped up inside the hypnotic slogan is either tautologous or too vague for verification to be possible. Just what kind of 'degree' is it, for that matter, that millions of Aspro-users keep finding themselves 'one under'?

It can be argued that the constant appeal to discreditable impulses of this kind is unlikely to have much effect except on those who are already abnormally susceptible. We may agree that it is the self-indulgent who will respond with most alacrity to slogans about chocolates with 'less-fattening centres', or to the stomach-powder manufacturer's encouragement to 'Eat what you like – without suffering for it'. On the other hand advertising agents are united in their conviction that sheer weight of repetition can be amazingly effective (hence the remarkably long life meted out to such slogans as 'Players Please' or 'Guinness is Good for You'); and it should be remembered that what we are exposed to is a combined assault by many different advertisers, all converging to direct their appeal to a small number of well-proved human weaknesses. Thus although it may be only the exceptional motorist who falls in at all fully with the implications of the invitation to 'Put a Tiger in your Tank', nevertheless this particular extreme example works in consort with a host of other advertisements for petrols, cars, and motoring accessories to establish an unquestioned assumption that what every motorist longs for above all (on our overcrowded roads) is speed, engine-power, and acceleration. Road safety is not apparently considered a strong selling-point for motor-cars.

This is perhaps a convenient opportunity to note that advertising agencies seem to be, in private, distinctly cautious in their estimate of their own persuasive power, preferring usually to follow the line of least resistance rather than seek to challenge or work against existing tendencies at all directly.* Thus motivational research revealed a few years ago that most people brush their teeth only once a day, before breakfast and therefore 'at the most pointless moment possible in the entire twenty-four hour day from the dental hygiene standpoint.'† The reaction of the advertising agencies, however, was not to undertake a campaign to persuade the public of the importance of brushing one's teeth after meals in order to minimize dental caries. Instead they accepted that the operative motive in using toothpaste is the desire to give a pleasant taste to one's mouth first thing in the morning, and therefore made flavour the selling-point in their advertising. Hence, the emphasis in much subsequent toothpaste advertising on 'clean

---

* Exceptions to this can be observed in some recent advertising campaigns in this country. In 1954 Fifty Shillings Tailors decided to change its name to John Collier, and to plug the theme of 'personal service' (every suit hand-cut by craftsmen) as a counter to the unfavourable 'mass production' associations attaching to multiple-tailors, and more recently Burtons have struck a similar note with advertisements for 'The suit that is *personally* tailored'. C. & A. (for Men) on the other hand have set out to attack the same prejudice in a slightly different way by urging you to 'Buy your suit the Modern Way' (i.e. off the peg). Another example of a direct assault upon an unfavourable 'image' is the emphasis upon freshness in advertisements for Lion-stamped eggs ('Fresh from the nest, etc.'); early complaints had had the effect of making it fairly widely known that normally the Egg Marketing Board collects from the producer only once a week.

† Vance Packard *The Hidden Persuaders*, p. 21.

mouth' and 'tingling taste'; later Colgates ('Children love its minty flavour') made even more irrational play with the same motivation in their slogan 'Brush before breakfast ... destroy bad breath ... fight tooth decay ... *all day*!'

For the most part, therefore, advertising acts (and is content to act) as a reinforcement of already existing tendencies, but even so it seems likely that the multiplicity of small pressures work together to effect significant shifts in the total pattern of socially-accepted values. In countless ways often unnoticed we are led to accept as common ground a world in which the key to happiness is the possession of the newest model of car, dining-room suite, refrigerator, and television set, in which any malaise can be neutralized by recourse to a branded anodyne or laxative, and in which the chosen reward for a hard day's work is to 'treat yourself' to a luxury you can't afford because you feel you 'deserve' it – or even 'owe it to yourself'. The picture of the good life thus built up is as notable for its omissions as for what it contains; books, symphony concerts, and art exhibitions, for instance, command no advertising budget. In general terms the verdict of the Pilkington Committee cannot be seriously questioned:

Since they [television advertisements] sell goods by holding up certain attitudes as admirable, it seems obvious that they are at the same time and to some degree 'selling' the attitudes also. Although there is no compelling statistical or quantitative proof of this, failing such proof the responsible course must be to assume that the attitudes and values which act as vehicles for the sale of goods are themselves also being 'sold'.*

The tendency to reinforce impulses which are socially undesirable is only part of the problem. Even more insidious may be the advertiser's growing ingenuity in linking his product with ideas and images which are in themselves innocuous, pleasurable, even commendable. In consequence of this the concepts of sexual love, manliness, femininity, maternal feeling are steadily devalued for us by their mercenary association with a brand-name – as though the real human values they

* *Report of the Committee on Broadcasting*, 1960, p. 80.

31

represent can be purchased by rushing out and buying a new shaving lotion, a new deodorant, even a new washing-machine. Mother-love seems to be the target most favoured by practitioners of this tactic, and the following example is only a little more nauseating than most of its kind:

When there's love at home, it shows. It shows in the smile of the mother who gives it. It shows in the happiness of her family who are secure in it. ... It shows in the fact that she chooses Persil for their clothes.

Children are notoriously photogenic, and the calculation is, presumably, that the smiling face of a toddler (preferably in colour) will generate enough initial goodwill to outlast the impact of such a punch-line as: 'Mother can you be sure? Can you be sure your children are getting enough body-building goodness?' – or even of so embarrassingly Barrie-esque a piece of dialogue as:

Mummy, who do you love best?
What a funny question!
Well, you don't give *me* that nice soap.
But baby's skin is very delicate ...
So is *mine*, Mummy!
All right, darling, you shall have Johnson's too ...

A similar estimate of our willingness to tolerate commercial intrusion into intimate corners of our personal lives is manifest in the glamorous photographs of young lovers with heads together in happy harmony over glasses of stout ('Jennie shared Neil's love of walking ... and his choice of drink'), or stretched out on a grassy bank to enjoy, in the intervals of courtship, a puff at their favourite brand of cigarette. In the following example, taken from a woman's magazine, the reader's eye is to be riveted first by the large and romantically-composed photograph and then led, by carefully selected typography and layout, through the skilfully-contrived verbal daydream to the final goal of the brand-name.

That magical summer,
he found love in a soft glance ...
a radiant complexion

Lovers Meeting

It began long ago ... with a letter in Sue's childish hand to her pen-friend Kim in California. She had quite forgotten Kim when years later a letter brought news of her and went on ... 'This is really to introduce my brother Pete. He's won a scholarship to study in your country and knows just no one there. Then I thought of you ...' and not long after, Sue heard, for the first time, Pete's deep slow voice on the telephone asking for a date. They met – and then again. His gentle manner, his disarming grin, soon made him a favourite with her set. Then, more and more, it was just she and Pete ... alone even in a crowd, in their own private world. One golden day by the river Pete asked Sue to be his wife. Close to her, Pete felt Sue's cheek, warm and soft against his. 'My, you're beautiful,' he whispered. 'When they see that English complexion back home ...' Sue is still as fresh and lovely as she was that day – thanks to Knight's Castile ...

Obviously an important human emotion is trivialized when it is thus reduced to a single commercially-manipulable aspect. (In this case the aspect chosen is that of simple physical attraction; a comparable effect can be studied elsewhere in the salesmanship which seizes on 'Entice' as the name for a perfume or which recommends chocolates through the medium of a slinky vamp thinking – or saying – 'I like a man who likes me enough to buy me Cadbury's Contrast'). Over and above this, however, we can observe the inherent compulsion to stereotype experience on a level which is rapidly and universally communicable, and hence to congeal the capacity for emotional response in forms which are even more standardized and constricting than the magazine fiction from which they derive. Here are feelings which have indeed been 'processed' to the uniform consistency and flavourlessness of a cheese spread.

Since the advent of television advertising in September 1955, the main weight of mass advertising has been transferred increasingly from the Press to the television screen. Expenditure on television commercials climbed rapidly to an estimated total of £83 millions in 1961, and a high proportion of this was spent by the manufacturers of a small number of heavily advertised commodities, such as soaps and detergents, cigarettes and tobacco, soft drinks, sweets and chocolates. Thus in 1960 tobacco manufacturers spent nearly £4½ million on television advertising as opposed to about £3,800,000 on Press display advertising. The specially-formed companies which make most television commercials can command lavish resources – the budget for a hundred feet of advertising film is reported to be higher than that available for making even entertainment feature films. They are able to call too upon the talents of many of the country's outstanding technicians and film-directors: witness the work of Lindsay Anderson for Rowntree's, of Karel Reisz for Persil, and of Joseph Losey for Nimble Bread. To analyse the methods used by advertisers in this evanescent medium is peculiarly difficult; words are no longer the main channel of appeal, but have become only one adjunct among many – the visual setting, the personality of the actors, the camera angles and cutting, the background music, the catchy singing-jingle, the appeal of the puppet figures or the amusement contributed by the animated cartoon. There can be no doubt that the combined effect of these multiple resources makes an exceptionally powerful impact. Moreover they blare out upon the viewer at a time when he is sitting at his own hearthside, comfortable, relaxed, almost defenceless; since they often appear unpredictably in the middle of a programme, the only way to escape them is to refuse resolutely to turn the knob of one's set to the commercial frequency. It is rash to generalize, since the medium makes it possible to combine a remarkable variety of different appeals within the space of a single forty-five-second commercial; but it would seem that the aggressive hectoring approach is giving way increasingly to more subtle forms of blandishment. The preferred aim nowadays is to associate the product with pleasurable screen images and personalities rather than harp on fears and anxieties that may introduce a jarring note into the family viewing. Cigarette brands are linked, by the most tenuous of connexions, with idyllic rural or sporting scenes, photographed in sunlight which is unfailingly benign; while a bedtime drink has to be extolled to us, in rapt tones, because it provides 'a *happy* flavour at the end of each day'. An unbridled euphoria must surely overtake any viewer who watches for long enough the succession of eupeptic faces smiling forth from spotless kitchens whence all effort has been banished and in which every mouthful that is tasted calls for an ecstatic coining of superlatives.

In recent years there has also been a marked stepping-up of the advertiser's traditional reliance upon appeals to irrationality; and this seems to be due at least in part to the nature of the television medium itself, where the director's multiple resources for influencing mood and atmosphere make it far easier to sidestep the sceptical reaction and to exploit to the full the power of unconscious and semi-conscious association. There is, however, a further important factor which has worked in the same direction. The standardization made inevitable by modern mass-production methods has meant that increasingly the most heavily advertised products are indistinguishable from their nearest competitors – apart from their brand-name. Few smokers, for example, can tell one make of cigarette from another by taste alone; while consumer reports have revealed little significant difference between the various brands of detergent, either in efficacy or in chemical composition. In this situation advertising agencies are led to concentrate above all on the emotional aura they can attach to their client's 'brand-image', whether by finding a new brand name, by giving a new colour to the package, or by exploiting some wholly irrelevant association which has been proposed by the motivational-research analyst. To the logical mind it may seem a doubtful recommendation for a breakfast cereal that it provides 'the fastest breakfast ever'; nor would any reasonable person choose one tin of soup in preference to another on the grounds that it had been 'tested' at ten o'clock rather than eleven. Nevertheless it seems that if such a claim is insisted on with apparent seriousness often enough, many people can be hoodwinked into overlooking the absurdity of it; the indirect effect of this in reducing our capacity for rational choice in matters of more moment for us than soup-buying will surely bear thinking about.

Brief mention should be made here of some other ways in

which advertising has lately adapted its methods of approach in response to changing patterns in the social environment. First, the insistent stress on 'newness' in current advertising. 'What's new in Colgate Dental Cream that's MISSING – MISSING – MISSING in every other leading toothpaste?', screamed one (American) advertising agency a few years ago ; and today we are constantly invited to be all agog at a 'new' soap, a 'new' detergent, an 'enticingly spicy new flavour' in a soup, 'an absolutely new kind of softness' in a toilet roll. 'Now-superb *New* packs' proclaims an advertisement for Wills's Whiffs – as though *this* was just what we had all been waiting for. This line of attack makes capital out of our layman's awareness that technological change in industry is going ahead today at an unprecedented rate. There are, indeed, genuinely advantageous new techniques for constructing automobiles, preserving food, synthesizing fibres, and so forth – though sometimes these advances have, in their early stages of development, attendant snags which are very little publicized. But much of the advertising that hammers away most noisily at this theme of 'newness' is concerned with modifications which are of very slight or even doubtful benefit to the consumer. Thus it seems, oddly enough, that the composition of a toilet soap may be modified from time to time in ways which are *not* widely publicized, after which the manufacturer will go to town in his advertising with an eye-catching but essentially non-significant variation which can only be described as a gimmick (the introduction, for example, of Lux in four pastel colours 'To mix! To match! To have fun with!'). In some cases the advertiser's obsession with 'newness' can be related also to an industry's decision to keep its mass-production assembly-lines flowing at a constant rate either by making the product less durable than it need be ('built-in obsolescence') or by continually changing its outward appearance so that last year's model soon looks old-fashioned ('annual styling').

The appeal of fashion is of course the favoured theme of much advertising directed particularly towards teen-agers and young adults. Two recent examples will suffice: one for a face-powder – 'The IN look is pearled translucence' (here a dash of pseudo-science has been added to the mixture); the other the slogan, linked with a series of photographs of well-known jazz performers, which informs us that PEOPLE WHO SET TODAY'S TRENDS DRINK Long Life CANNED BEER (an interesting example this of the way in which changing patterns of social prestige have installed the television or entertainment-world personality as the contemporary inheritor of the snob-appeal formerly wielded by a testimonial from the Countess of X). It should be noted that marketing studies carried out in the past decade have revealed that young people between the ages of fifteen and twenty-five dispose of a remarkably high spending-power. According to Dr Mark Abrams, Britain's five million teenagers spent in 1959 no less than £830 millions, the average boy spending 71s. 6d. a week, and the average girl 54s. A high proportion of this money goes on a fairly narrow range of consumer goods (particularly clothing and footwear, tobacco, drinks, sweets, cosmetics, records, magazines); and in consequence some manufacturers have seen an advantage in angling their advertising to catch this teen-age market. (Notable examples at different times have been Rowntrees, Skol Lager, Babycham, and Players, Strand, and Bristol cigarettes; some of the collective advertising of the Brewers' Society has also had the evident intention of rehabilitating both beer and pubs in the eyes of young people, though not specifically of teen-agers.) One motive for spending big money on advertising for this age-group is the hope, often justified, that 'brand-loyalty' once established may last for life; and the same argument applies with even more force to advertising directed at children. Understandably enough most parents would prefer to be able to choose their breakfast cereal on its own merits and not on account of the balloon or toy bullet inserted inside the packet; and they are inclined to feel some resentment at the attempt to put pressure on them indirectly through such slogans as 'Don't Forget the Fruit Gums, Mum!' Moreover it seems wrong, to many adults, that immature minds should be subjected to unscrupulous psychological manipulation for commercial ends. There may be little reason to believe that children are notably more susceptible than their elders to direct pressure from the admen;

but since their attitudes and outlook are still in process of formation, there seems little doubt that they are exceptionally vulnerable to the indirect influence upon values and standards discussed above, and the massive weight of persuasive advertising to which they are at present exposed seems bound in the long run to stereotype and debase the quality of living of future generations.

'PAY THE PIPER, CALL THE TUNE'

Propagandists for advertising make much of the fact that advertising revenue enables us to watch television free of charge and to buy newspapers and magazines at a price considerably below the sum which they have cost to produce. The 'fact' is itself slightly mis-stated. We do, of course, have to pay the full price, in the end, for our papers and television programmes – by means of a small impost every time we buy detergents, cigarettes, petrol, or toothpaste. Moreover, this indirect form of compulsory levy reduces the power of each one of us to decide what he will pay for, and how much he will pay for it. I can choose whether or not to subscribe towards the cost of the BBC's programmes through the purchase of a television licence; but we all have to contribute our annual quota to finance the 'Independent' Television channel, whether we possess a television set or not.

These subsidies which advertising pays on our behalf add up to vast amounts. In 1961 the television programme companies received from advertising revenue some £64 million net. In the same year about £215 millions was spent on all forms of Press advertising, of which some £73 million went to national and London evening newspapers, £55 million to the provincial newspapers, £39 million to magazines and periodicals, and £33 million to trade and technical journals. It is more difficult to estimate the net financial gain to the Press, since a newspaper has to pay for the paper and ink needed to print the advertisement, and also to staff and maintain its own advertising department; but it seems safe to say that at least half the total advertising revenue can be regarded as a net subsidy. If there were no advertising it is likely that we would have to pay about 5d. for a popular paper which now sells at 3d. and about 7d. for a quality paper which now sells at 4d.

The main effect of this dependence on advertising can be stated very simply. Advertisers want their advertisements to reach as many people as possible; they pay for space in newspapers at the rate of so much per column-inch per thousand readers, and they pay for time on commercial television according to the number of captive viewers they can count on having delivered to them. (In autumn 1961 Associated Rediffusion charged £770 for a fifteen-second spot during the peak viewing-hours of 7.25 to 10.35 p.m., as compared with £235 between 5.25 and 6.55 p.m.) The overriding aim of the media-owner must therefore be to secure for his advertisers a guaranteed mass-audience. Newspapers, magazines, television programmes are in any case already fantastically expensive to produce; the initial outlay (on equipment, machinery, personnel) has to be spread over a very large number of readers or viewers if there is to be any possibility of profit. The influence of the advertiser steps up a little farther the already-compulsive drive towards a mass-audience – an audience numbered not in thousands, or hundreds of thousands, but in millions.

Where numbers are what really count, the inevitable tendency is to pull them in by playing safe; by sticking to tried and tested formulas which appeal to the lowest common factor in every one of us; in general, in fact, by concentrating on those forms of entertainment or items of news which promise the maximum immediate titillation in return for the minimum effort. Unless it be very late at night, when the audience will be relatively small anyway, no commercial television programme can afford to appeal to a minority – not even to those sizeable minorities which care for opera or ballet or Beethoven or Shakespeare. The fate of the *News Chronicle* in 1960 showed that nowadays even a million readers are not enough to keep a daily newspaper alive.*

* Exceptions to this are the handful of quality papers which get by with a circulation of only a few hundred thousand. Because they have a high proportion of middle-class readers with above-average purchasing-power

The snag in all this is that universality of appeal is not quite the same thing as popularity. A newspaper or magazine which 'has something for everyone' may be bought by millions and yet give little real satisfaction to any of its readers; the television programme which fewest people switch off may yet be keenly enjoyed by no one. The need to approach us all as units in a mass involves inevitably a levelling-down in the general standard of taste – a studied avoidance of the areas of experience in which we live most fully, either as individuals or as members of a group sharing a common passion or enthusiasm; a drift instead towards the inertly conventional triviality which is utterly without character but for that very reason antagonizes no one.

Dependence on advertising moreover implies a subtle distortion of purpose, in that the paramount need is to please the advertiser rather than to satisfy the reader or viewer. The entertainment or the page of print comes to be judged in part as a setting for the advertisements which border it (*they* after all are what bring in the profits). This consideration certainly determines presentation, as one may know when trailing a magazine-story through its devious trickle, flanked all the way by brand-names, from page seven to page seventy. It may also influence content, though the relationship is necessarily more elusive in this country than it has sometimes been in the United States, where commercial sponsors have been known to abandon a programme series because it provoked too much suspense or too much laughter for their purpose. (One can see that it might be better business to frame one's sale-talk with a mildly hypnotic panel-game rather than have it drowned by amused comment on the vagaries of *I Love Lucy*.) Even here where direct sponsorship has been excluded, one may doubt whether the advertisers would remain content for long if the entertainment provided by the programme companies were markedly

---

they are able to charge above-average rates for advertising space. For the most part only a limited range of advertisers find it worthwhile to pay these rates – manufacturers of luxury cars and central heating equipment, for example; there is also a certain amount of prestige advertising designed to keep a firm's name in front of the directors and executives of other firms.

more absorbing than the commercials which punctuate it every thirteen minutes. Certainly one often has the impression that the advertisements and the bait which accompany them are remarkably similar both in ethos and in surface appearance. In particular, one may suspect an ulterior motive behind the prevalent bonhomous atmosphere of synthetic optimism; isn't this the mood in which the advertisers think we're most likely to part with our money? One recalls the sponsor who once told a leading American television impresario* 'in a wonderful phrase delivered with a completely straight face that what he wanted was "happy shows about happy people with happy problems".'

Easier to illustrate, of course, are the more trivial manifestations of the power of the advertising manager – the editorial puff for the advertised product, the special supplement concerned with holiday travel or with some particular industry, the colour section shrewdly constructed according to the space salesman's specification in order to tap for the *Sunday Times* certain new sources of advertising revenue. And deference to the susceptibilities of advertisers also shows itself in two negative respects, which are rather more important. It inhibits most newspapers from any attempt to review critically ordinary commercial products in the same way that they review books or films. And it ensures that one will never hear, from either Press or commercial television, any radical criticism of the advertising industry itself, however much this might be in the public interest.

THE ECONOMIC ARGUMENT

In 1938 two per cent of our national income was spent on advertising. This proportion dropped sharply during the war, but has risen steadily in the post-war period to an estimated 2.2 per cent in 1960. European countries spend less proportionately on advertising than we do, but the comparable figure for the United States has now reached the neighbourhood of three per cent. Another way of looking at these figures is to

* David Susskind, quoted in *Power Behind the Screen*, by Clive Jenkins.

compare the annual amount each country spends on advertising for each member of its population. A 1961 survey estimated this at 62.60 dollars per head in the U.S., 27.20 dollars in Sweden, 21.60 dollars in Great Britain, and 16.30 dollars in West Germany. The indications are that the more prosperous a country becomes the more it spends proportionately on advertising, though which is cause and which effect is a moot question. The probability is that the proportion of our national resources which we in Great Britain devote to advertising (already high comparatively) will continue to increase in the future.

It is obvious that the individual manufacturers who allocate resources to advertising believe that this improves their sales and increases their profits, although their grounds for this belief can seldom be of a kind which would satisfy a social scientist seeking meticulous proof. (Advertising agents are inclined to claim any increase in sales as evidence for the efficiency of their advertising campaign, although in reality advertising is only one among a large number of factors that may have been at work. It is significant that a recent study by an economist reported that: 'The attempt to discover the reasons why firms spend particular amounts on advertising proved fruitless. ... Most firms which expressed an opinion thought that they were spending too much on advertising but had to do so because their competitors did so.'*) The question we need to ask, however, is: 'What are the social benefits which accrue from the expenditure to society at large?' One claim customarily advanced is that advertising reduces prices to the consumer because it makes possible the economies resulting from mass production. Here too it is very hard to isolate the influence of advertising as such; but some instances can be cited which disprove the general contention. Thus *Shoppers' Guide*, summer 1959, reported the case of a kettle, the price of which had been raised from 23s. 1d. to 37s. 6d.; when questioned, the manufacturer wrote: 'An extensive national advertising campaign is being conducted on it.... This increase in price is

* T. Barna *Investment and Growth Policies in British Industrial Firms*, 1962, p. 24.

mainly due to the advertising charges.' In the same year a manufacturer of raincoats gave an account in a letter to the *Guardian* of discussions he had had with an advertising firm with a view to entering the field of branded goods. If the proposal had gone through, the cost of advertising would have meant an increase in price to the consumer of nearly £1 (about fifteen per cent), whereas the maximum possible saving by way of reduced overheads as a result of increased production would have been a matter of coppers. Some multiple stores have shown that it is perfectly possible to achieve mass-production economy with either negligible or very moderate advertising, and at the same time to sell a thoroughly sound product (e.g. Boots' Anti-Freeze) at a price much below that of expensively advertised competitors. We might quote also the launching by J. Bibby in 1960 of an unadvertised soap, Coronet, which sold at 7d. a bar as against 9d. to 11d. for most other brands, and quickly built up a sale of four million bars a year.

Certainly it may be true that when a genuinely new product is launched (ball-point pens and synthetic detergents are often cited as examples), heavy initial advertising is necessary in order to build up a mass market quickly. Detergents, however, have continued to carry massive advertising long after the point at which they became fully accepted by the housewife; and in this case at least a reduction in the advertising budget, reported to have amounted at times to as much as 6d. on a 1s. 11d. packet, could have resulted in a useful price-cut to the consumer. Indeed, in spring 1962, Unilever decided to try the experiment of offering *Surf* in packets guaranteed to contain eighteen per cent more washing-powder for the same price as before, but with no premium offers or competitions, and a greatly reduced advertising allocation; curiously enough, Unilever's other washing-powders are still being sold, in competition with *Surf*, by the same gimmicks which have aroused so much resentment among intelligent housewives.

In the case of washing-powders, heavy advertising has been the main weapon in a prolonged trade-war in the course of which the two giants, Unilevers and Hedleys, have virtually carved up the market between them. A number of studies have shown the extremely wide variation between different products in the amount of advertising they carry. Thus the ratio of advertising expenditure to turn-over may be as much as twenty-two per cent for patent medicines and cosmetics (1958 estimate). On the other hand, although expenditure on advertising all alcoholic drinks reached in 1959 the vast total of £16-18 millions, the turn-over was also so large that this represented only three per cent of total sales. Kaldor and Silverman in their thorough study of British advertising in the year 1935 concluded* that the extent of advertising was related not so much to the nature of the commodity as to the number of manufacturers competing for the market, advertising being heaviest where there was fierce competition between a fairly small number of large advertisers. There are grounds for thinking that this analysis could be shown to be equally valid in relation to advertising today. Toilet soap, toothpaste, sweets and chocolates, breakfast cereals, ice-creams, refrigerators are all heavily advertised products, the market for which is divided between a handful of very large firms. In such cases high advertising costs tend to act as a barrier against the entry into the field of new competitors and at the same time to enable the existing firms to maintain both prices and profits at a high level. Thus, although world prices for maize have fallen by twenty-five per cent since 1956, the price we pay for the breakfast cereal manufactured from it has remained steady (at least 1s. 1d. for eight ounces as compared with under 3d. a pound for the raw material). When a new competitor has enough capital to pay the heavy entrance-fee, advertising expenditure may soar even higher for a time. Thus, a few years ago the British soup market, then dominated by Heinz, Crosse & Blackwell, and Batchelor, was invaded first by Knorr-Swiss (later bought up by an American firm, Corn Products) and then by the American giant, Campbell Soups; and advertising expenditure rose rapidly to over £2 million a year. In such conditions it is hard to see how advertising can bring any price benefit to the consumer,

* N. Kaldor and R. Silverman *A Statistical Analysis of Advertising Expenditure and o the Revenue of the Press*, C.U.P., 1948.

either during the fiercely competitive 'oligopolistic' phase or at the later stage when one firm has succeeded in establishing a near-monopoly.

More plausible superficially is the argument that we live in a large-scale industrial society which is subject to constant technological change and in which mass-produced articles have to be brought to the consumer through increasingly impersonal channels of distribution. In such a society advertising is necessary in order to keep the consumer informed about new materials, new gadgets, new ways of living (some apologists would even say 'to create new wants', though it is hard to see how a want can be very important if it has to be persuaded into existence). Certainly there is much we need to know when we set out to buy a drip-dry shirt or have to make up our mind between linoleum and vinyl for our flooring; and we commonly find that, even when we keep away from the self-service shelves, the shop assistant is in no position to help us since the only thing he knows about his wares is whether or not they have been advertised on the telly. The information we require is often complicated; even the lucidly-presented pages of *Which?* or *Shopper's Guide* do not always make it easy to master. By contrast the information contained in advertisements is minimal, and what there is is suspect. *Suggestio falsi* is regarded as a legitimate device, and we are in for disillusionment if we suppose that a statement that 'Bakers eat it' (a branded loaf) means that someone has conducted a survey of bakers' bread-eating habits. Brand advertising as we know it today is, in fact, geared not to rational decision but to impulse-buying in the supermarket.

A further argument advanced for advertising is that it increases total consumer spending, and thereby helps to create a high level of employment and general prosperity. In so far as this is true (and most economists would regard the case as 'not proven') the effect is accompanied by a distortion in the *pattern* of spending which goes far to nullify any benefit which you or I might feel in our own living. This can be seen particularly clearly in relation to the free gifts and 'premium offers' which have proliferated so enormously since the mid 1950s, largely under American influence. Apart from the illusion of having obtained something for nothing, are you really any 'better off' when you have received a plastic rose attached to your detergent packet, or have purchased a wobbly ball at a cut-rate by sending a postal order accompanied by two packet-tops? The 'premium offers' are sometimes (though not invariably) good value for money, since direct buying in large quantities enables the manufacturer to offer his silver-plated teaspoons at a price lower than that in the retail shops, yet without much cost to himself. (Many of the offers are, in fact, 'self-liquidating', and cost the manufacturer nothing so long as they sell out.) But clearly these offers, particularly when directed at children, must tempt many families to divert money away from a genuine need to the purchase of an article which is not much wanted and may in the event be little used. Similarly with the national budget, since it is often inessential goods (confectionery, cosmetics, cigarettes) which are the most heavily advertised, and in any case the incidence of advertising is determined not by any criterion of public good, but by the state of competition existing within the various industries.

Professor J. K. Galbraith has pointed out that in the United States 'advertising operates exclusively ... on behalf of privately produced goods and services'; the result is a social imbalance between privately-produced goods and publicly-supplied services which he has trenchantly characterized as a contrast between 'private wealth' and 'public squalor'. In Great Britain the dichotomy is less obvious, since the nationalized industries do advertise to a moderate extent (both for directly commercial and for prestige reasons), and there is also a small amount of 'educative' advertising on behalf of public health and accident prevention. Nevertheless the trend over the past decade has undoubtedly carried us some way towards a reduplication of the American pattern. Our eyes and our ears are constantly assailed on behalf of more beer, but not more schools, more laxatives but not more hospitals, more sweets to be eaten between meals but not a more adequately staffed school dental service. And although Government policy has been the main culprit, the pattern of advertising has surely done much already to accentuate the currently-alarming 'imbalance' between private and public forms of transport.

WHAT REMEDIES?

The increased volume of advertising over the past decade (and in particular the licensed appearance since 1955 of fireside hucksters in every home) has produced an unmistakable upsurge of public irritation and uneasiness. One public opinion poll for instance showed that sixty-one per cent of those interviewed were 'annoyed a lot' by commercials in the middle of television programmes. In 1958 a debate in the House of Commons led to the formation, the following year, of the Advertising Inquiry Council, an unofficial non-party body which sets out to represent the interests of the consumer in advertising. The AIC now publishes a monthly bulletin *Advertising Scrutiny*, and has done useful work in acting as a watchdog on guard against specific abuses by advertisers. Extreme cases of misrepresentation in advertisements are already subject to restriction in certain fields by legislation and more generally by the voluntary 'codes' operated by the Advertising Association and by the Institute of Practitioners in Advertising; but there is still scope for public pressure to insist that these codes should be observed in spirit as well as in the letter. It was presumably in response to such pressure that the Advertising Association decided in May 1962 to set up an Advertising Standards Authority to promote and enforce its own codes; it may be felt, however, that such an authority would command more confidence if it consisted of lay representatives and not of spokesmen for the different advertising interests.

In relation to the wider issues it is tempting to put one's faith in education, and to hope that as fresh generations grow up to be more discriminating and critically-minded in their reading, viewing, and spending, the mass-persuaders will be compelled to raise their sights and to reduce their reliance upon cheap emotional manipulation. Certainly there would be more chance of this happening if time could be found before they

47

leave school to alert all teen-agers to the nature of the appeals which will be played upon in order to wheedle their first earnings away from them. And from one point of view, the need for some inoculation of this kind has become the more urgent now that the techniques of commercial advertising are being used increasingly to mould public opinion by pressure groups of all kinds, not excluding political parties and even governments.

It is sometimes suggested that, if only it could be sterilized, as it were, by the need to woo a more critically-minded audience, advertising might develop into a beneficial cultural agency disseminating to a wider public the visual idiom of the modern artist and designer. There is scant substance to this myth, and precious little that one could point to as supporting evidence. In the early days of colour-lithography some artists of distinction (notably Toulouse-Lautrec and the Beggarstaff Brothers) were sufficiently excited by the new medium to design some highly attractive theatre posters; more recently London Transport has sponsored underground posters which are not at all bad to look at, and which may have had some effect in enticing travellers to visit places of interest near tube stations. But apart from a few highly untypical instances of this kind, advertising makes contact with significant movements in visual (and cinematic) art only to the extent that it extracts, for its own purpose, elements and motifs which have already degenerated into clichés. Moreover its purposes are such that, in thus following a 'movement' at several removes, it also inevitably debases and vulgarizes it even further. There are no 'good' advertisements, only 'effective' ones. In this field, in fact, education must always be negative ('education *against*'); and in these circumstances we must not expect too much from it, or be surprised if its results are slow to show themselves.

In the meantime there is one other approach which ought to be explored. Far too much money is lavished at present on consumer advertising – far more than any economic argument could justify, even if the indirect damage to our cultural life is left out of the calculation. Much of it is spent, moreover, by

48

a limited number of large manufacturers: The *Financial Times* reported in 1960 that half the advertising time on television was taken up by no more than twenty companies. Part of the trouble is that the whole of a firm's expenditure on advertising can be deducted as an allowable expense before computing the company profits which are liable to income tax. There seems to be no valid reason why a ceiling should not be set to this allowance, in rather the same way that an individual is limited to claiming two fifths of his life insurance premiums as an allowance against income. If firms had to bear a proportion of the expense of their advertising out of profits, they would be inclined to scrutinize their budgets more carefully; and some might find it would pay them better to put money into improving their product rather than into buying goodwill for their brand-name. It may be that as an indirect consequence the profits of the television companies would diminish, and we would find ourselves paying a more nearly-economic price for our newspapers and magazines – but even then how many people outside the advertising industry would feel moved to complain?

*

BOOKS

LIONEL BIRCH, *The Advertising We Deserve?* (Vista Books, 1962)

MAX CORDEN, *A Tax on Advertising?* (Fabian Society, 1961)

ELIZABETH GUNDREY, *Your Money's Worth* (Penguin Books, 1962)

RALPH HARRIS AND ARTHUR SELDON, *Advertising in Action* (Hutchinson, 1962)

MARTIN MAYER, *Madison Avenue U.S.A.* (Penguin Books, 1961)

VANCE PACKARD, *The Hidden Persuaders* (Penguin Books, 1960)

DENYS THOMPSON, *Voice of Civilization* (Muller, 1943)

PHILIP ABRAMS

I am watching 'Tonight'. Some burly women are taking part in a wood-chopping competition. 'This,' says a jolly voice, 'is the way to solve your winter fuel problems. But they'll have to work faster than that.' The film speeds up. The women, all wearing ridiculous shorts, scurry to and fro ridiculously. 'That's the spirit,' says the voice. The film goes faster and faster. Thirty seconds later we have switched to high seriousness – a grave interview with the authors of a new book on international armaments. Three minutes later there is another change of mood. Now we are asked to consider the struggle of the Nagas to win independence. In fact we learn rather little about this struggle as the peg on which the episode is hung is the sentimental tie between the Nagas and a Scottish lady who lived among them and who now talks about their sterling qualities and great charm. The story is illustrated with unidentified pictures of nameless people shooting each other. When I next look up it is to see the Minister of Transport riding his bicycle.

It was for programmes like this that the Pilkington Committee whitewashed the BBC. I would not suggest that the distinguished viewers and listeners who gave evidence to the Committee were wrong to sense a great gulf of quality between the service of the BBC and that of the independent companies (although none of them seem to have watched at all systematically); but even the BBC is, as programmes like the one I've just watched make clear, the victim of certain inherent tendencies of the broadcasting media. These are tendencies towards what the Pilkington Report calls 'trivialization'. I want to suggest that such tendencies are built into the very nature of British broadcasting and that it is in the context of such tendencies that one has to try to evaluate 'good' and 'bad' programmes. In any medium one can judge quality only in terms of the technical limitations and possibilities of the particular form of communication in question. In the case of broadcasting I would argue that the process of trivialization, or what we might call the 'law of optimum inoffensiveness', is to a large extent integral to the technical nature of the media and not something that needs to be explained in terms of the wickedness, bad taste, or financial greed of particular men who happen to be in charge of the media.

But to say that in British conditions the tendency towards trivialization is virtually a technical fact of life for radio and television is to state a problem, not to solve one. Within the limits set by the law of optimum inoffensiveness better and worse programmes are still possible; it is necessary to ask what, given those limits, broadcasters can do well and what they ought to leave alone. And here we at once come upon a peculiar characteristic of broadcasting among the mass media – the belief of broadcasters that they can do everything, that theirs is a medium supremely suited to *all* forms of communication, and consequently that they should do everything. In fact there is a direct relationship, or so it seems to me, between the excessive pretensions of broadcasters and the trivializing effects of broadcasting. 'It's all the same, I don't enjoy it any more; it's boring' was the way one viewer described his experience of television to one investigator. If this seems a sad comment on a medium of which the proudest boast is that it brings 'Life' to the people, it is perhaps worth asking whether it is not the undiscriminating attempt to transmit 'Life' as a whole that is responsible for the blurring of identities and differences that such comments betray. Might it not be that just because these media try to do everything, try to 'hold a mirror up to society', try to compete with all other forms of communication, broadcasters lay themselves open to charges of triviality and that they themselves find it so difficult to realize their other professed aim, the aim of 'raising' standards of public taste?

This, essentially, is the problem I want to explore. It can be reduced to three main questions. How far and in what ways are tendencies towards trivialization an intrinsic part of what we might call the working logic of these media? Should and can radio and television cope equally well with all forms of communication, and if not for what sorts of communication are they best suited? Within these limits what ought we to mean by 'good' and 'bad' and the other evaluative noises we apply to radio and television programmes of different sorts?

The simplest description of the broadcasting media will spell out the nature of their working logic. We may go on from there to consider the implications of the way the media are organized for the way the media perform. Radio and television have four qualities which distinguish them from all other mass media. They are universal, continuous, public services for domestic consumption. Each of these characteristics has consequences for what broadcasters do and have to do and hence for the content of the programmes they provide.

Universality, the fact that these are media for all the people, is perhaps the most consequential element of the four. British broadcasting, in the words of the Crawford Committee in 1926, was to be 'conducted by a public corporation acting as a trustee for the national interest'. This notion of a national interest persists (it was presented to the Pilkington Committee by many witnesses for example) and it equips the broadcaster with a quite crippling image of his proper relationship to his public. From the first, one service, from one source, through one channel has been the official ideal. The coming of independent television increased the number of sources but, ironically, it left the theory of the system unchanged. It is a system organized from the centre on the assumption that there is a basic uniformity of tastes throughout the community and that the best way to provide broadcasting for the community is therefore to make sure that the same material, selected at the centre, reaches as many people as possible. Special outlets for special groups or interests, a 'Hyde-Park' conception of broadcasting, with many communicators speaking to many minorities, were never seriously considered. Instead we have created a 'School-Prayers' system of broadcasting with one headmaster addressing all the boys. Bodies of dignitaries are set up to preside over the

media and make sure that all tastes are represented in the programmes. But unfortunately it is easier to dilute interests and
tastes than to represent them in their full variety and inconsis-
tency in a system like this. If one insists on universality in the
sense of communicating to every one from one source for as
much of the time as possible, representation is bound to give
way to dilution.

And this of course is what has happened. The media have
steered an unswerving middle course between every kind of
authentic idiom. Among current programmes we have 'rebel-
lious' teenagers singing 'respectable' middle-aged songs; we
have detectives quite evidently incompetent to detect their way
through an 11+ I.Q. test, Westerns to which the historical reality of the West is irrelevant and serials about working-class
life in which working is the one thing people hardly ever do, in
which class never rears its ugly head, and in which life is one
long laugh; we have had, too, brand new satirical programmes
in which Pope's 'strong Antipathy of good to bad' showed
signs at once of giving way, as the occasion for mockery, to
a 'good for a giggle' view of life, in which the technique
of Swift who 'lashed the vice but spar'd the name', gave way
to the technique of Frost, who, as it were, 'dropped the name,
but spar'd the vice'.

In short, the universality of broadcasting puts the media in
a false relation to society. They are impelled to treat as homogeneous what is in fact a tangle of more or less dissimilar
groups. The decision to provide a single service of programmes
of universal appeal could in practice only be a decision to work
in terms of an artificial 'Highest Common Factor', to standar-
dize the content of the media at a level of maximum acceptability. Success, related to the ideal of universality, means the
largest possible audience for each programme; size can be and
usually is pursued regardless of programme content; hence, no
doubt, the dilution of 'That Was The Week That Was' from
something like an authentic political cabaret to something increasingly like one more variety show.

BBC and ITA have recognized the necessity of evolving a
single contrived idiom around which their programmes can

cluster in different ways, but each has recognized it. For the BBC it was a matter of overt policy so far as radio was concerned; the object, as the Director General put it, was 'that one general policy may be maintained throughout the country and definite standards promulgated'. Independent television, on the other hand, acknowledged the logic of universality more obliquely. The only commitment recognized in the Television Act of 1954 is the commitment 'not to offend public taste'. The Act gives no clue as to whose opinions are to be taken as constituting 'public taste'. In practice it has become clear that it is 'official' opinion that the ITA most respects, while for the rest it strives to achieve a state of 'balance' in which as few people as possible will actually be offended by anything transmitted. Thus we have the withdrawal of a Granada programme on Defence policy on the one hand, and a 'popular' idiom, as contrived as the BBC's 'respectable' idiom, pervading ninety-nine per cent of programmes on the other. BBC television, beginning life as a new embodiment of the 'respectable' mode, has, in the face of competition, rapidly adapted to the 'popular'. Perhaps the most worrying finding of recent surveys has been the demonstration of how *little* difference there is, programme for programme, between BBC and ITA.

Neither the principle of 'one general policy' nor that of 'no offence' has much to do with respect for public taste or for what might be called socially or culturally 'authentic' standards of discrimination. The meaning of the two norms for the content of what the media communicate is perhaps clearest in the styles of speech they have developed. Two 'media languages' have been created. We have the 'BBC accent' on the one hand, colourless, formal, the perfect representation of Lord Reith's 'definite standards', and 'mid-Atlantic', the language of the disc-jockey and the advertiser, equally stilted, equally unrooted in English usage, on the other. Each represents a stunting obliteration of personality for the sake of maximum acceptability. Each is a part of the price broadcasting pays for its commitment to universality of communication. Each was justified, before the Pilkington Committee, in terms of an ideal of cultural democracy.

The desire to be democratic within the technical framework set by the media – very wide coverage and very few channels – does raise real dilemmas, of course. The problem is often presented as a choice between minority and majority interests. I prefer to see it as a choice between standards of authenticity on the one hand and of acceptability on the other, between programmes that respect felt boundaries of taste and discrimination among the audience and programmes that ignore such boundaries for the sake of a larger, albeit less satisfied, audience. The 'democratic' course, it is often argued, is obviously the latter. And as a result we have programmes like 'The Adam Faith Show' and 'That Was The Week' – teenage music engulfed in whimsy, satire deadened by jollity. In such a situation no one gets programmes that are perfect for them but everyone gets programmes that are more or less tolerable.

My own feeling faced with arguments of this sort is that in matters of culture and communication the only meaning one can give to the idea of democracy is authenticity. The notion of a homogeneous mass audience which can be given what 'it' wants, is, in broadcasting, thoroughly misleading. Democracy in a one-way structure of communication can only mean respect, first for existing differences of group interests and tastes within the audience, and second for the nature and limitations of the material being communicated. For this reason only some few sorts of programmes are capable of being given universal appeal without diluting or compromising their subject-matter. Basically these are programmes of a 'documentary' type so far as television is concerned; and as I shall argue later it is for documentary communication (using the phrase in a rather wide sense) that television is best suited. In the same way the technical nature and limitations of sound radio equip it to transmit music and news in ways that combine universal appeal and authenticity. In all other respects so far as these media are concerned the acceptable and the authentic ought to be thought of as mutually exclusive goals, between which it is the broadcaster's job to find some honest compromise.

In this sense there is only one group for whom radio and television even begin to operate democratically at present. Ironically it is the highbrows, especially musical highbrows, who are thus favoured. It would be absurd to quibble over the standards of performance of the Third Programme; in providing access to music and discussion for people living too far from London to have any chance of experiencing these things at first hand it realizes perfectly the literal purposes of broadcasting; and it does so without any compromise of standards. Here the media have singled out a meaningful and coherent sub-section of the total audience and the broadcasters concentrate on maintaining a flow of communication only to that sub-section. The result is a triumph of mass communication; it is mass communication from which the concept of the mass has been eliminated.

But excellent as it is that the BBC should have broken the grip of universality on broadcasting, this setting aside of special channels for special audience groups is a solution that raises as many problems as it solves. Lord Reith objected to the idea of a Third Programme on the ground that with the intellectuals set aside the doctrine of universal acceptability would gain new strength in the main body of programmes; that when concessions to intellectual standards no longer needed to be made it would be assumed that no other differences within the audience mattered. And his fears seem to have been well grounded. In the wake of the Third Programme sound radio introduced the 'magazine' programme, the scrapbook collections of fascinating bits and pieces, oddments of information, whimsical tales, tunes, and jokes, no item lasting more than a minute or two, making no demands on anyone, offering something for everyone. And the television equivalent of these radio rag-bags, the so-called 'family' programme, monopolizes the main viewing hours in the same way – programmes in which the doctrines of universal appeal or 'no offence' find their apotheosis. With the highbrows set aside (given the Third Programme by radio and the last hour of broadcasting by television) both media have become more frankly devoted to substituting the acceptable for the authentic so far as all other groups are concerned.

The hiving-off of the highbrow audience has also served to

lend weight to the idea that the only way to escape from the problem of universality, the dilemma of acceptability or authenticity, is to segregate particular audience groups. Given the nature and cost of broadcasting this may indeed be the case. If so it is not so obviously desirable a solution as to be a welcome alternative to present practice. One other possibility would be that the media might use the time available to them more aggressively; they could provide a succession of programmes each designed for a distinct and different minority taste within the total audience; in this way they might confront the audience with constant contrasts in standards without either diluting any particular standards or making it too easy for any particular group to lose contact with other groups.

Here we come upon the second basic characteristic of the broadcasting media, their continuity. And at present it must be said that the way broadcasters use their special advantages of time serves to aggravate not modify the implications of the doctrine of universal appeal. Not only are these media expected to provide communication for all the people but they are expected to do so more or less all the time. The BBC has now announced plans for broadcasting into the small hours. And so long as the highest common factor of acceptability or 'balance' is the guiding norm of programme policy the fact that radio and television function round the clock will surely mean that we have more and more of the same thing. The guiding light in the planning of BBC2 has been, quite plainly, the principle of 'more of the same'. The only advance in discrimination has been the discrimination between days of the week; 'Friday night is family night'. It is difficult to recognize in what we have been offered so far the 'flexible and adventurous' channel we were promised. The constraints of acceptability seem to have clamped down on adventure.

Uniquely among the mass media radio and television are given opportunities by time, by the fact that they have the whole day, every day, to dispose of, and that they can break up the day as they please. How do they use these opportunities? We tend to take the existing pattern of programming so much for granted that we do not see the gulf between what could be done in this respect and what actually is done. Time, which might have been used to experiment and innovate, to set contrasting styles and idioms alongside one another and so heighten audience sensibilities, has in fact been used only to reproduce with endless ingenious but minor variations programmes built on established formulae of acceptability. With its new lease of time the BBC proposes to fill the night air with 'light music'; even the American radio companies are willing to treat the small hours as a time for experiment and for special minority interests. In this country the continuity of broadcasting means that the onslaught on authenticity has become unremitting; there is always something 'on'; and the essential nature of what is on is, for almost all of the time, unchanging.

The fact of continuity thus serves to compound the trivializing tendencies of universality. The whole experience of viewing or listening is turned into a glorified version of 'Tonight'. And the point about a programme like 'Tonight' is that item follows item too smoothly and rapidly for any one item to engage the attention or grip the imagination for more than the moment of its passage. Comical items and serious items, the calamitous and the diverting parade before us in unending processions. No pause for thought or differentiation is allowed.

The same is true for broadcasting as a whole. Because something must always be on it is virtually impossible to give different weights to different items. Unless one decides to switch off to think or talk in the split second between items or programmes one's chance of absorbing or digesting, let alone criticizing, what one sees or hears is lost. It is a standard feature of the reports of people who have 'observed' groups watching television that incipient comment or conversation about a programme is quashed as attention is drawn back to whatever next appears on the screen. Discussion gives way to asides and appreciative noises. The effect is of a blurring of edges, an ironing-out of differences of stature and scale between items and programmes. Individual programmes share the fate of the heroes of Webster's play:

> These wretched eminent things
> Leave no more fame behind 'em, than should one
> Fall in a frost, and leave his print in snow –
> As soon as the sun shines it ever melts
> Both form and matter.

In broadcasting the sun of the next programme is always shining. Within ten seconds of a tribute to Bertrand Russell there follows a tribute to Ivor Novello.

A single evening's fare will make the point. Family viewing-time opens with a thirty-minute Western, then for five minutes we are shown the effects of an earthquake in Persia – the loss of life in both programmes being about the same. Then we have a fireside chat with Lord Robens, a serialized slice of working-class life, some ballroom dancing, a quiz for cash prizes, a little ballet, a few words with a doctor about drugs liable to produce deformed babies, a few words with a spokes-man for the pharmaceutical industry to redress the balance, football, a murder mystery, and so to bed brooding over the weather forecast. In the middle of all this there are scraps of news, and, for those with the strongest digestions, equally scrappy advertisements. Continuity in this sense reduces the world to a music-hall. Programmes are poured at us without distinction; they run together, wrapping the audience in an eiderdown of unreality; they blend in ways which serve, as Raymond Williams puts it, 'to deflect, postpone, and cushion any relevance to actual living'. 'It's all the same, I don't enjoy it any more ...'. Actually, of course 'it' is not all the same; that is simply an effect created by radio and television.

And these effects are compounded again by the third characteristic of broadcasting, its domesticity. It is this characteristic that makes it virtually impossible for radio and television to escape from the tendencies to trivialization which their universality and continuity encourage and permit. Radio and television are provided in the home. And because they are one does not have to make any conscious act of choice in order to be exposed to them. To see a film one has to decide to go to the pictures (not necessarily to see the film one sees, though). Reading a paper or going to a football match or a pub all involve a relatively deliberate effort; one chooses what to do and what should happen to one. None of this is true for watching or listening. These are activities on which one embarks, typically, unthinkingly; they are so easy to embark on. People can and do switch on in a way that is as routine as the way in which they wash and have tea when they come in. These are activities from which the problem of decision has been removed. 'Now,' as one man put it, 'you don't need to worry how you will spend your time.'

Ever present, radio and television provide alternatives, not just to other activities, but to the whole problem of thinking what to do. One BBC survey found that the more an individual watched television the less likely he was to describe himself as 'choosey' rather than 'not choosey' about the programmes he watched. And this is not very surprising. Because television is so easily available it is given functions which have nothing to do with conscious choice or cultural discrimination. For people who watch a lot it is not just what they watch but the fact of watching that is important. There seems to be a direct progression in this respect from the 'choosey' ten per cent at one end to the ten per cent of 'addicts' at the other extreme for whom watching and listening have become rewarding activities in their own right regardless of what is seen or heard. Most people are not in either of these groups of course and do discriminate to a greater or lesser degree. But the domesticity of broadcasting, combining with its universality and continuity, opens a primrose path along which the audience has an open invitation to be led towards addiction.

In one particular way the domesticity of broadcasting furthers the decline of choosiness. Because programmes are so easily and constantly available one thing that most members of the audience are likely to ask of the media sooner or later is that they provide a certain minimum of wholly undemanding distraction. Radio and television are asked to do things which other, non-domestic, discontinuous, selective media cannot – to allow listeners and viewers to relax, to provide just the sort of 'cushion against reality' that Raymond Williams describes, to create an agreeable background for passing and wasting time. Because they are domestic these media are expected to be unexacting, to provide relief from routine and effort. Nor do I see how this demand, even if we call it a demand for 'escape', can be said to be unreasonable or improper. The quality and pace of modern work make it difficult to censure the use of broadcasting for light relief. Broadcasting, in short, through its special character, acquires strictly non-aesthetic, social, and psychological functions which other media do not have (or do not have to nearly the same extent). R. H. S. Crossman, indeed, goes so far as to speak of a 'right to triviality'. Certainly, a non-stop supply of programmes making rigorous demands on the judgement, attention, and imagination would deny to most viewers and listeners an important and proper use of the media.

And if the demand for background is legitimate it follows that some provision should be made in an ideal scheme for it to be met. A good deal of what is communicated by these media not only is ephemeral (as a result of the 'one transmission only' norm of broadcasting performance which is itself a by-product of universal coverage), but ought not to pretend to be more than ephemeral.

But to ask for space for the light-weight is not, of course, to endorse a flight from standards of authenticity even in light-weight programmes. The fact that the media are used for 'escape' makes it more not less important for us to have clear criteria for judging the goodness or badness of the material that is used in this way. One possibility is suggested by the sociological literature on the mass media. In this literature increasing attention is being given to the uses people make of the media and to possible side-effects of those uses. It is suggested for example that while one may use television to escape from tedious or vexatious situations of one's daily life, there may also be a 'feedback' from the material one uses for escape to the way in which one subsequently sees and handles the situations of 'real life'. What the nature of this feedback will be seems to depend not on how far the individual uses the media for escape but rather on what the escaper finds *in* the material he uses. The feedback from some media or some programmes may be narcotizing but from other media or other programmes one may gather resources of understanding and sensibility which contribute creatively to one's 'real' social relationships. To consider one obvious dimension of this problem; a serial may be narcotizing or invigorating for those who view it as 'escapist' to the extent that it disregards or respects individual personality. In this sense *'Coronation Street'* perhaps qualifies as a 'better' serial and *'Maigret'* as a 'worse' one; though the former caricatures life it deals in consistent and constantly enriched personalities; the latter, despite the novels from which it is drawn, shows no sense of personality and deals in stock types and contrived situations.

In short, to speak of a 'right to triviality' is not to give a licence to the trivialization which seems to be the broadcasters' own favourite solution to the problem posed by the demand for background, for media that function as occasions for 'escape'.

But the problem remains. How can media with universal coverage and a limited number of channels, continuous broadcasting and domestic consumption meet the need for 'background', a need felt by different people at different times and in different ways, without compromising the standards of authenticity and respect for divergent tastes which in principle one wants to demand of them? Perhaps the problem is insoluble so long as British broadcasting is organized as it now is. Perhaps some limited compromises are inevitable. But it is ironic that at present the fourth and last basic characteristic of these media, their public service status, should also contribute powerfully to the tendency towards trivialization. Not only is trivial material easier to provide than authentic material (making fewer demands on the energies and imagination of already harassed broadcasters), but the official mythologies of British broadcasting themselves favour triviality.

The BBC is, and ITA has convinced itself that it is, an 'established' not to say an official institution, with appropriate commitments to respectability, impartiality between interests, and apparent self-effacement. Both like to see themselves as above controversy and party strife. Both are dedicated to the ideal of providing services in the 'national' interest, services

of information, education, and entertainment. Both are sensitive to complaints about their objectivity. Both profess aspirations to help in the 'raising' of standards of public taste; at the
same time both express concern to cater for every taste, to
'hold a mirror up to society' and whatever happens not to
'impose' on public opinion. Both seek to be fair to all points
of view. Both want above all to be democratic, responsible,
impartial.

Both are thus in a cleft stick of their own making. On the one
hand they are anxious to lead or raise standards of taste. On
the other hand they will not countenance anything that can be
criticized as 'imposing' on taste. I have already suggested that
perhaps this democratic dilemma is a false one. In a one-way
system of communication one cannot help imposing on taste.
Even a programme like 'Listeners Answer Back' is, in effect,
shaped unilaterally, by the producers. A mass communication
system of this kind can never have the flexibility, the reciprocity
of conversation. Mass communication is a gift not an exchange.
The only real question is what shall be imposed; how and by
whom shall the messages be pre-determined?

At the same time, one cannot lead taste if one has no sense
of direction; one cannot raise standards unless one will allow
that some things are better than others and some worse. And
what has happened with these media is that the public service
image of their own role has made broadcasters so afraid of
imposing that they do seem to have lost all sense of direction.
In its place they have set up a largely spurious public service
ideal of impartiality. Other mass media may have the wrong
values; one's first impression of radio and television is that
they have no values. The Press and cinema may glamorize
the shoddy and they may have false, even vicious, priorities.
But at least they have priorities; they do patently select and
editorialize; some things are headlined and some ignored; if
a newspaper felt like flaying the government's Defence policy
it would do so; it is sensible to talk about the 'character' of
these media. Radio and television, on the contrary, have no
editors, they do not take stands, they do not admit to having
conscious and consistent principles of selection – except

perhaps the worst of all possible principles, the principle of 'news value'. The Pilkington Committee had a hard time getting the controllers of these media to admit that they ever chose or planned anything. What the broadcasters offered the Committee were the ideas of neutrality, balance, and the mirroring of society.

Such ideals mean different things for different types of programmes; in so far as it is necessary and desirable for radio and television to function as universal public services it would seem to follow that these media ought to concentrate on those sorts of programme to which the ideal of impartiality is most appropriate (especially as, for other, technical, reasons, these are the sorts of programme which these media do best in any case). I shall return to this point shortly. First, a word is perhaps in order about the ulterior arguments on which the whole working logic of the media, as I have described it, is premised. These are the arguments about democracy, respecting public taste, and 'giving the public what it wants' which I have touched on several times already and which were made articulate by both BBC and ITA in defending their present practice and their commitment to impartiality to the Pilkington Committee.

Arguments about giving the public what it wants are the over-arching claims in terms of which all the trivializing tendencies of the media are drawn together and collectively justified. Like the belief in impartiality the appeal to what the public wants is spurious through and through. Just as something has to be selected and something rejected whether the selecting is done consciously or not, so the highly centralized structure of broadcasting means that judgements are constantly being made about the nature of audience-wants and that in practice the only test of these supposed wants is audience size. And I would suggest that to defend programmes that are more 'acceptable' than 'authentic' on the ground that such programmes have huge audiences and that these huge audiences show that such programmes are what the public 'wants' is to ignore the real relationship that exists between the broadcaster and his public and to make nonsense of the idea of a want.

Gilbert Seldes, in one of his essays on the mass media, tells a story of a cinema proprietor in Nigeria who owned, and showed, only two films, *King Kong*, and *The Mark of Zorro*. Three days a week he packed the house with one of these; on the other three he did the same with the other; on Sunday as a surefire double feature he showed them both. This went on for years. The story epitomizes the relationship between communicator and public in the mass media. This enterprising man had fastened on to a *general* demand for entertainment; this he had met in a somewhat specific way; and he had gone on to work up an audience for the specific form of entertainment he was able to provide; finally, since he monopolized the means of entertainment in that region, he had contrived to 'prevent an audience for any other sort of entertainment from coming into existence'.

The sorts of demands people actually make are diffuse and unspecific. If one asks what 'want' a particular programme is meeting one very rarely finds that the want is one that could be met *only* by the programme in question. Rather, general wants, for amusement, background, excitement, are met in the particular ways the broadcasters find most convenient. The relationship between communicator and public is a manipulative one with the initiative firmly on the side of the communicator. When television provides a glut of Westerns the public selects Westerns as its favourite type of programme; when the companies switch to providing hospital dramas the public discovers a want for these. A series of recent studies has shown with growing clarity how far, as Dr Himmelweit puts it, 'taste is the product of the producer, rather than television entertainment the response of the producer to the public's taste'. Or as Gilbert Seldes writes:

Demand is generalized and diffuse – for entertainment, for thrills, for vicarious sadness, for laughs; it can be satisfied by programmes of different types and different qualities; and only after these programmes have been offered is there any demand (specifically) for them. Supply comes first in this business and creates its own demand.

The nature and working logic of these media tend, in short, 'to

65

create those conditions in which the wants that can be most easily satisfied by the communicator take precedence over others'. And what this means in practice is that tendencies to trivialization are built into almost everything that the media do. This is the easy and convenient way to operate; to some extent even the unavoidable way.

Trivialization is, at heart, a simple failure to treat the subject one is handling, whatever it may be, with the respect it deserves. A programme, as the Pilkington Committee point out in what is perhaps their most important single argument, is not trivial because its matter is light or unimportant; it is trivial if its matter is devalued in the process of communication:

Triviality resides in the way the subject matter is approached and the manner in which it is presented. A trivial approach can consist in a failure to respect the potentialities of the subject matter no matter what it be, or in a too ready reliance on well-tried themes, or in a habit of conforming to established patterns or in a reluctance to be imaginatively adventurous ... in a failure to take full and disciplined advantage of the artistic and technical facilities which are relevant to a particular subject, or in an excessive interest in smart packaging at the expense of the contents of the package, or in a reliance on gimmicks so as to give a spurious interest to a programme at the cost of its imaginative integrity, or in too great a dependence on hackneyed devices for creating suspense or raising a laugh or evoking tears.

I have quoted this passage at length for it provides the best brief statement I know of the nature of the problem that is built into the organization of television and radio in this country and of the sorts of tests we ought to apply to broadcast material.

British radio and television are beset with the problem of trivialization. As I have several times suggested, the things these media can do best are the things in which the difficulties of trivialization are least urgent. Broadcasters themselves tend to believe that broadcasting can do anything. Specifically the media exist to provide services of three kinds, services of information, education, and entertainment. In effect, where-ever the broadcaster tries to fill the first or second of these roles the chances are he will succeed and that radio and television will prove superior media of communication to most others; wherever he tries to fill the third role, that of entertainer, the chances are he will fail and that radio and television will prove less adequate media than many others.

In trying to decide what these media can and cannot do we must, then, start by setting aside the delusions of communicative grandeur created by the universality, continuity, public service status, and technological ingeniousness of broadcasting. The built-in tendencies towards trivialization which I have been discussing are evidently of the kind to make the worst impact on any programmes designed primarily to entertain, programmes to which purely aesthetic criteria are most directly relevant. It is in the quality of such programmes, for example, that the impact of the domestic demand for agreeable background and the effects of the spurious belief in impartiality in programme selection are likely to be felt most. My first argument for seeing these media as channels primarily suited to educative and informative tasks is thus a negative one.

The one outstanding exception is music; here radio, but not television, remains a perfect medium; not so much for the quality of reproduction or performance but for the range of music to which the listener is given access. This of course is the fruit of a deliberate policy decision. It was a decision which has given sound broadcasting an unchallengeable and distinctive function among the media. One could complain in this respect only of the fact that so much broadcast music is still of the vacuous 'light-classical' variety – and here of course one runs up against the problem of the need for 'background' and the assumption that 'background' material has to be intrinsically worthless. Personally I suspect that Vivaldi could be played as acceptably for this purpose as Leroy Anderson but we are dealing with a 'supply-creating-demand' situation here until someone makes the experiment. Television, on the other hand, does not seem suited to the transmission of music; either the camera gives a head-on view of an entire orchestra so reduced in size as merely to strain the eyes and infuriate the intellect; or it roams around providing normally an arbitrary sideshow to the music; in either case it is an unnecessary and distracting addendum to the music itself. There is, again, one exception, however. Television is an admirable medium for solo performers. It does not add anything to the quality of the music of course and may again distract attention from the music itself. But it does permit a scrutiny at close quarters of a performer's technique; it gives us something over and above the sheer sound and this is something that it is valuable to have. But what it does is essentially of a documentary nature; is shows how music is made; it permits us to understand a craft; this is a real aid to appreciating the music in itself.

Television, however, is an admirable medium for talks; here the visual element is typically exploited in ways that complement and enhance what is being said. As compared to radio where the normal limit for a talk is nineteen minutes, it being calculated that listeners cannot concentrate for longer than that, in television devices of illustration have been developed which focus attention for much longer periods, and which in the hands of at least some producers do support and not distract from the talk itself. Basically, this is an educational or informative activity of course. When someone has something to say, whether it is sixth form physics lesson or why we should join the Common Market, and television's visual devices for making points are mobilized in a disciplined way to help him say it, this medium emerges as a surely unparalleled means of effective communication.

The same is true for all programmes of the 'live documentary' type – interviews, news programmes, sport, discussions, straight documentaries on controversial subjects, expositions of seemingly difficult matter (such as John Freeman's extraordinary and brilliant programme on the human brain) – for all these purposes television is in principle and by virtue of its special technical facilities highly suited. Such programmes should be judged by the most rigorous standards so far as trivialization and authenticity are concerned. They are the sorts of programmes where television is capable of excellence; triviality of the sort that occurred in the edition of 'Tonight' I mentioned at the beginning of this chapter has no excuse in this field.

Similarly whenever television treats entertainment in a basically documentary way – as when it gives us not only music but a close study in musical technique, or not only ballet but a scrutiny of the detailed skills of dancing – or when it creates entertainment out of documentary matter – as it has done in popularizing show-jumping and swimming and interior decorating – it is again potentially at its best. In all these contexts of course the standards of greatest relevance are technical and then moral, not aesthetic ones; what matters is how effectively points are made, how relevant is the technical apparatus to what is being said; how fair and thorough is what is said in relation to its subject-matter; how honest and uncompromising is the presentation. In this sense a programme like 'What the Papers Say' is, in the hands of an uninhibited reporter whose own standards of criticism are clear, perhaps the highest form of communication to which this medium can aspire. Not only is information of some public importance effectively communicated, but a contribution is made to the discussion of public issues and a public hitherto excluded from such discussions at any influential level is given access – if only as spectators – to the arenas in which public issues are decided. Television functions, as the Press once functioned, to create and maintain an informed and politically relevant public opinion.

It is when its attention turns to art or simple entertainment that broadcasting steps beyond its natural territory. Here the limitations of universality, domesticity, and the ideal of impartiality make themselves felt most brutally. Consequently, it is in this field that broadcasting is least likely to do well but also in this field that one has to make most allowances for broadcasting – since the reasons for its shortcomings are so largely built into its organization. Nevertheless it is here that directly aesthetic appraisals are most relevant and it is to such evaluations that broadcasting is most vulnerable.

The basic trouble with television drama, for example, is to my mind that the psychological relationship between viewer and performance is wrong. It is a relationship that destroys the stature of what is being performed. For some reason – perhaps simply because the distancing effect of a proscenium arch is so enormously aggravated – television contrives to reduce the scale of the drama both physically and emotionally to the size of a puppet show. The alternative, of course, is to make heavy use of close-ups and to select plays in which the exploration of personality is paramount and collective situations and group action subsidiary. Even so television, and still more sound radio, simply because it is one dimensional, seem to me intrinsically less satisfactory media for drama than either the theatre or the cinema. Everything about television militates against a play acquiring dramatic stature. In the first place the producers and performers know that what they are doing is ephemeral in the extreme; television plays have one performance only, they do not aspire to be more than momentary entertainments. I can believe that it requires at least some sense of the possible permanence of what one creates to sustain an endeavour of aesthetic merit. Secondly, the television play is not presented or viewed as a unit but as an item in a mixed programme of an evening's entertainment; here again the theatre and cinema gain in that the play or film is offered as an isolated event, a work in its own right. Even a television play of the type most suited to the nature of the medium, a play of personality in which there is some true psychological complexity, labours under these difficulties. And the sense of the need for universal appeal, domesticity, and the provision of 'background' all probably reduce the chances of such plays being put on in any case.

But what especially impairs television drama and other broadcast entertainments is the very mythology of impartiality that contributes so much to the high standards broadcasting achieves in its documentary activities. In the latter the ideal of neutrality is a source of strength of course. If one compares the radio or television handling of any news item or controversial issue with the performance of the Press, or of the so-called 'news' provided in the cinema, it is clear that these media have the highest journalistic standards in the country. And there is evidence that the superior reliability of broadcasting as a source of information is widely recognized by the public.

People are more likely to 'trust' radio and television than other sources of news; and they are right to do so. In matters of education and information the ideal of impartiality is broadly relevant – especially when it is taken in the sense of the present Director-General of the BBC as meaning 'neutrality between Left and Right but not for a moment neutrality between Right and Wrong'.

In the third area, the area of entertainment, it is not so much impartiality as commitment that is needed, however. As I have suggested, in this area the nature of the media makes any attempt not to impose on taste unreal. Aspirations to cultural neutrality merely conceal from both the communicator and the audience the nature of the imposition. The 'holding a mirror to society' argument masks an act of evasion, not of responsibility, a refusal to discriminate consciously behind which there must lie unconscious discrimination, intuitive selection taking the place of purposeful and critically articulate selection. The fact that the criteria of selection are not brought to light – for fear no doubt of the charge of paternalism – does not mean that selection does not take place. However seemingly casual, random, and value-free, however plausibly explained-away as 'what the public wants', selection of material for broadcasting by the broadcasters is inescapable. And the criteria of selection become the implicit, unspoken values of the communicators. Since purposeful selection in the field of entertainment is deplored the basis of selection is seldom scrutinized. But it does not take much study of the content of broadcast entertainment to discover behind the seeming neutrality a persistent, no doubt unconscious, diffusion of a distinct, and not very agreeable, view of life.

In the absence of other criteria the style, idiom, and values of radio and television entertainment are set, in practice, in part by the unstated values of the communicators, in part by the working logic of the media as a whole, in particular by the pursuit of universal appeal and what that is taken to mean. The nature of the ensuing 'media values', and the extent to which they mould the attitudes at least of younger viewers, have been forcibly demonstrated by Dr Himmelweit and her colleagues. On a modest scale one can quite easily repeat for oneself the sort of experiment that allowed her to disentangle and identify these media values running through different entertainment programmes. It is useful to repeat such scrutinies of the norms of broadcast entertainment, for through them one comes to appreciate just how much selection, how much predetermining of the supposed 'mirror-image' of society is in fact involved in broadcasting. There is for example the consistent presentation in television drama as normal and desirable of what is in fact 'essentially an urban and upper-middle class society' ... 'essentially the ideology of a competitive society'. The viewer is offered a world in which 'the most important qualities for success are determination and will-power; kindness and unselfishness are of lesser consequence.' Purporting to reflect the world the entertainment offered by these media offers a definition of the world which is not the world known to most people and which rests on values alien to most people and certainly alien to the professed ideals of most educators and public men.

In evaluating television and radio entertainment one should, then, not only make certain allowances for the commitments of the media to universality, domesticity, etc. One should also have some conception of an ideal broadcast entertainment which would be one that both escaped from the unconscious commitment to 'media-values' into some more articulate and desirable commitment, and used to the full the special facilities of these media for entertainment – facilities for the intimate as opposed to the spectacular, the detailed as opposed to the grandiose, subtlety and precision and a sense for the texture of personality as opposed to glamour and brashness and a surrender to what F. R. Leavis has called the 'illusion of technique'.

In all these respects broadcasting as a medium of entertainment lags far behind broadcasting as a medium of information and education. Yet it is still for entertainment rather than information or education that both communicators and audiences are most dependent on and most devoted to radio and television in Britain. Documentary broadcasting is constantly 'spiced up' under this pressure.

BOOKS AND PUBLICATIONS

Report of the Committee on Broadcasting, 1960 (H.M.S.O., 1962) – an invaluable statement of the aims and organization of radio and TV and a development of the idea of 'triviality'.

H. T. HIMMELWEIT *et al., Television and the Child* (Oxford, 1958) chapters I–IV have been published separately as a pamphlet summarizing the findings of this book – the most important and conclusive body of research on the content and effects of television that we have.

M. MASHEDER, *Family Viewing* (Council for Children's Welfare).

Facts and Figures About Viewing and Listening (BBC, 1961) – a useful collection of data about audiences which makes the point, among others, that audience size and programme popularity are not at all the same thing.

B. PAULU, *British Broadcasting in Transition* (1961).

H. H. WILSON, *Pressure Group* (1961) – a study of the television lobby, its motives and sponsors.

Independent Television Programmes; facts and figures (ITA).

R. H. S. CROSSMAN, 'Thoughts of a Captive Viewer' (*Encounter*, August 1962) – on, *inter alia*, the 'right to triviality'.

The Journal of Social Issues, no. 2 (1962) – a special issue of an American journal on 'The Uses of Television', with articles by H. T. Himmelweit and Raymond Williams which bring their respective books up to date, and an important general survey by Gilbert Seldes.

The Public Opinion Quarterly – perhaps the most useful of the more technical journals, it usually has one or more pieces of fairly substantial research on the nature, effects, and evaluation of television and radio in each issue.

New Society – among the more general periodicals has to date had an excellent record so far as keeping up with research and discussion on broadcasting is concerned.

UNESCO, *Screen Education: Teaching a Critical Approach to Cinema and Television* (1964) – excellent essay, setting out the problems of cultivating a discriminating approach. Suggests standards of judgement and exercises for comparing and evaluating programmes.

4   The Press

GRAHAM MARTIN

Plenty of people will try to give the masses, as they call them,
an intellectual food prepared and adapted in the way they think
proper for the actual condition of the masses. The ordinary popular
literature is an example of this way of working on the masses. ...
But culture ... seeks to make all men live in an atmosphere ...
where they may use ideas, as it uses them itself, freely, – nourished
and not bound by them. This is the *social idea*; and the men of
culture are the true apostles of equality.   MATTHEW ARNOLD

1

The Press* is by far the oldest of the mass media, and a com-
pressed survey of its modern workings ought to find this maturity useful. The sheer size and complexity of each medium,
and above all, their elusiveness as a subject matter makes short
treatment particularly hard. The Press is a subject neither small
nor simple, yet its age ought to have given it shape and definition,
to have familiarized the problems, and sensible ways of discussing them. Nevertheless, the Press cannot, in fact, be separated from the flux of popular culture any more easily than the
other media. The fact of its history has not protected it from the
contemporary pressures everywhere else in evidence – from
changes silently imposed by the multiplying alternative ways
of transmission, by the fact of these, as well as by the new styles
and conventions which disseminate from them. Thus – is it any
longer useful to talk in the old way about the Press in 'its political role' without taking in the contribution of radio and tele-

* Defined in the Oxford English Dictionary as 'periodical literature
generally', a useful reminder of the variety of publications that could here
be dealt with; but the term will be confined to its usual compass – daily and
weekly newspapers and journals.

vision news programmes? Or is it really worth while saying anything about the Press 'as an entertainer' without grouping it with modern magazines, with the general increase of visual over verbal contents, accelerated by the growth of photographic art, by the growth of films, and, again, of television? It is not only economically that the Press is now intimate with other media. From the cultural point of view, the continuity it seems to keep with its dignified past can be misleading and though we may still hear about the 'liberty of the Press' – the famous slogan on the famous banner – the people now waving this are very unlike the radicals of the 1790s or, indeed any radicals. Many of these changes and most of this inter-action with the other media has occurred within the last thirty years, some within the last fifteen. Should not precisely these ramifications into the media as a whole be the theme of this chapter?

As a subject-matter, then, the Press is just as elusive as the other media. But what of the methods which have become the established ways of treading the maze? Here, perhaps, is the framework within which the proportions of the subject can be fairly measured. It would be comforting to think so. Two standard, and nearly exclusive, approaches have emerged which can be called, shortly, 'historical' and 'literary'. Historical treatments conceive the Press as a quasi-political institution. From its beginnings in the Civil War (Milton the tutelary god), they trace its battles with government in the eighteenth century, its full emergence on the political stage in the nineteenth and certain degenerations from this ideal condition during the twentieth. The literary treatment, on the other hand, though it often depends on this history for some of its conclusions, starts from a different point. It sees the Press as part of a whole cultural condition, quite often as symptom of a cultural disease. (Arnold's phrase for journalism 'literature in a hurry' stands for an attitude that preceded and has survived him.) The contents of newpapers are held to wield the same kind of influence over mind and imagination as literature itself. The analytic and judicial skills of the literary critic therefore apply, and a discussion of the Press becomes an analysis of representative pieces of writing, of their likely effects, or of what they tell about the state

75

of mind of their writers or readers. Why will neither of these well-tried approaches serve here? Partly because one needs both, and partly because of certain shortcomings each has shown. As usually practised, historical discussions have three disadvantages: they treat only certain kinds of publication and so are factually incomplete; they tend, like much 'institutional' history, to narrate a too-simple progress, as if the Press had somehow enjoyed substantial autonomy from other relevant social processes and conditions; and the controlling definition of the Press as adjunct of the developing political structure is too narrow. (These points have been compellingly brought home by Raymond Williams in *The Long Revolution*.) The result is that a sound historical perspective on the present scene is not so much difficult as impossible. The usual literary analysis is affected by this, since it always presumes some history, but it has two further disadvantages of its own, particularly relevant to the discussion of popular culture. First, it simplifies the relationship that exists between the contents of the Press and the readers. Its model is the relationship between serious literature and equipped readers, with all that this implies of attentive open-mindedness and readiness of response. (In theory.) While this may hold approximately at some levels – and, since 'approximately', open the way to error – it is more and more misleading in these quarters where the issue of popular culture is most urgent. Secondly, it tends to identify the whole state of a reader's mind with what he reads, to allow only this reading as evidence. Certainly, it *always* matters what people read, but the written word is not the only, or even the main determinant of attitudes and values in most lives. The contents of newspapers do not impinge upon passive minds – we should be able to say this even without the supporting evidence about the complex ways people are in fact known to assimilate, select from, and reject 'communications' from the media. Finally, there is one objection to both approaches: they are apt to abstract the modern situation from the determining political and social context, as if – to cite one important result – real changes could come about within the Press alone. Yet even the partial history we have shows how close is the link between developments in the nature of the Press and in society as a whole. There is no reason to suppose that the future will be different.

The following discussion attempts therefore, though sketchily, to relate the styles and contents of the different products of the Press to their social role; and to bear particularly in mind that the society itself has ways of preparing its members for a certain kind of newspaper. If our newspapers fail to discharge their traditional function, or if they indicate a cultural wound, the key to this lies not only, or even primarily, in the newspapers, but in the society which makes use of them. (Any changes would of course come up against the fact that much of the modern Press is a reactionary social force – and in a much more stubborn way than is indicated by citing the predominance of 'conservative' opinion.) How, then (to begin with theory), is the social responsibility of the Press, or 'Presses', conceived? Everything depends here on who provides the definitions, but the main division of opinion is firmly established. On the one hand, there is the 1949 Royal Commission's well-known judgement that 'in our opinion the newspapers, with a few exceptions, fail to supply the electorate with adequate materials for sound political judgement'. It is here taken for granted that the main business of the Press is political, and that it carries out its duties by disseminating information about appropriate events, and by sustaining regular debate on their meaning. In direct contrast: 'surely the amount of uplift you can fit into any popular medium has got to be kept pretty low.' The speaker is Cecil King at the NUT Conference – the sentence is typical of his style of mind, which repays study – and the clear assumption is that the main business of the Press is not to 'uplift', but to 'entertain' its readers in ways they are known to enjoy: melodrama, gossip, sport (a kind of melodrama), exoticisms, 'titbits'. Neither of these definitions mentions money, yet a newspaper's attitude towards this is always illuminating. Political papers, which try to meet the requirements of the Royal Commission, want to make money in order to survive as political papers. 'Entertainment' papers, on the other hand, entertain in order to make money. This is to

describe ideal types, to which few newspapers wholly correspond, but they provide a frame for analysis, and most papers
recognizably tend one way or the other.

2

The political role of newspapers is the best known. Most
judgements of newspapers take this as their starting point. It
dominates the Press histories, and as a tradition claims the
famous names. The newspaper as 'entertainer' is nearly as old,
but it is less well known, and a good deal less approved. The history of the newspaper as a commodity is much shorter than
these, and is only beginning to be recognized as a distinct phase
that needs to be explored in detail. This is not, of course, because money-making played no part in the earlier phases. It
did, but in a subordinate position. The aim of the early 'entertainers' was as much to achieve cultural recognition as to
make money. Similarly, while Thomas Barnes' *Times* supported
political reform in the 1820s, grew in circulation, increased its
advertising revenue, and became commandingly prosperous,
its political role remained, and it was the mid-Victorian
editor, J. T. Delane, who gave this role its classic definition.
In contrast, Northcliffe's *Daily Mail* of the 1890s was not directed at readers with political sentiments needing a public
voice, but at a newly-arrived market of consumers ready for
the appropriate cultural commodity. Northcliffe's ambition
was to make money, and to do it he had to attract advertising. He therefore aimed at a large circulation, at the earliest
possible moment, which he regularly announced. The politics
of his paper, as the style and other contents (for 'tomorrow's
£1000 a year man, so he hopes and thinks'), were those that
would sell; or more exactly, and bearing in mind a modern
case of the newspaper as a commodity, those that would not
obstruct selling. ('We do not sell any copies on our politics' –
Cecil King, speaking of the *Daily Mirror*.) The interplay of
these different purposes – serious politics, entertainment, money-making – tell a good deal about any newspaper. If primarily
a money-maker, we should ask why a paper's readers seem

not to worry about politics. If primarily a political paper, we should look at the sources of its income, or lack of income. This usually shows why the paper can or does concentrate on the political role. It can also tell something about the actual politics: today's *Guardian* on the one hand, and *Tribune* on the other; or the post-1832 *Times* in contrast with Hetherington's *Poor Man's Guardian*, '... a weekly newspaper for the people, established contrary to the law to try the power of Right against Might'.

'A People are free in proportion as they form their own opinions', wrote Coleridge in 1796; and 'In an enslaved state, the Rulers form and supply the opinions of the people'. The political role of newspapers developed from an attempt to free (some of) the people from having their opinions formed and supplied by their rulers. In practice, this came to mean three things: accurate, independent, and timely reporting; sustained commentary and debate which, in given papers, followed a consistent political direction; and the strict separation of the one from the other. This is the tradition most people think of when they talk about 'a serious newspaper', and modern examples are usually discussed in intellectual or moral terms – balanced, discriminating, accurate, principled. But these qualities still take their energy from the political context in which they began, and they may be usefully conceived as laying down certain rules of communication between a paper and its readers which permit the latter to form – in a meaningful sense – *their own* opinions. When the rules are broken, the newspapers, like the rulers they originally displaced, begin to 'form and supply the opinions of the people'; (and in the modern situation, Coleridge's *supply* is prophetic). There is no need, in this discussion, to understand 'political' too narrowly. 'I regard the newspaper as a service ... for people whose obligations extend beyond their immediate circle' stated Roy Shaw at the NUT Conference, a definition which usefully shifts the emphasis from 'freedom' – the standard nineteenth century goal – to 'obligation'. But even obligations to one's immediate circle – food, health, housing, education, play – are inextricably political today; quite apart from those that go beyond it.

Ideally then, and to some extent in practice, serious newspapers exist in a continued tension with government. They seek out and publicize facts government may prefer to hide; they explore muddles and injustices; they analyse events and government actions independently of the pressure of intrigue or expediency, though usually from a particular point of view. This commentary may be offensive to reigning governments, and is always likely to disturb them. Some material may seem concerned with questions of no immediately-recognizable bearing on politics. But inspection usually reveals potential or long-distance political import. Much contemporary scientific reporting comes under this head. The political effectiveness of a newspaper depends on conditions that it does not directly control: notably a certain political structure. As recent history in Turkey and France shows, where this structure is imperfect, a serious newspaper's operations are hampered: censorship, confiscation, fines, imprisonment of editors follow as a matter of course. Without going into the details of this structure (it is hardly enough to transcribe the magical sign 'Democratic'), two things appear to be necessary. One is various political rights like those of assembly, and of the ballot-box. The other concerns the readers, and is best approached by way of that common description of serious newspapers as 'responsible'. This, despite the portentous stereotype it probably evokes, contains an important truth. A 'responsible paper' will address itself to 'responsible readers'. What does this mean? A responsible person is one who is answerable for his decisions and acts, either directly to others, or if to himself, then on behalf of others whose claim upon him he fully recognizes. Responsible government is similarly answerable for its record. A 'responsible' newspaper is rightly so called because it associates itself with government by seeking to influence the decisions government takes. Its readers are 'responsible' in the same way: they identify themselves, albeit critically, with the process of government. The education of the readers – an education of the emotions as much as of the mind – must fit them for this part. The most radical criticism of government is as 'responsible' as the most zealous support, because it invites readers to think of themselves as being, or as intelligently supporting, an alternative government. The only 'irresponsible' criticism a paper can offer is one that ignores the need in any collective for taking and holding by decisions, and answering for them. 'Responsible' has collected several other meanings, but this is the important one, and the habit of making it synonymous with 'preserving the *status quo*' should be resisted. As applied to readers, it should be taken to refer not to mental or emotional make-up, but to their relation to government; to, above all, the fact that they have, or feel themselves to have, a significant relation to government. It follows from this that 'irresponsible' readers lack this relationship.

This throws some light on the traditional practice of a serious newspaper: true facts, reasoned commentary, distinct from each other. From these it follows that newspapers, readers (and even if only formally, governments) recognize that certain intellectual and moral rules are necessary to political health. 'Responsible' derives its subsidiary meanings from these rules. But the root meaning of 'answerability' explains the peculiar stress laid on the separation of fact and comment. It is not simply that 'responsible' readers like to see the evidence from which comment is being drawn. The facts must be true and distinct because, quite apart from any editorial comment they may get, they are in themselves significant. To the 'responsible' reader, these facts indicate a reality with which he feels himself to be related. He can understand it, initiate further exploration of it, put the various bits together in his mind. He can – and this is crucial – act upon it as a result of what he has been told. Whether he will act, or when, and what the action will be (voting is not the only possibility) are questions which cannot be generally answered. Lord Home, Cruise O'Brien, a Conservative M.P. in a marginal constituency with a Liberal standing at the next election, a sixth-form student of nuclear physics about to sit a university scholarship will each act in different ways and at different times after reading a report about another United Nations military build-up in

Katanga. What they share, however, and it is this that makes them 'responsible', is a disposition to act upon information of this kind.

The history of serious newspapers shows this relationship between readers and the political world of relevant happenings which the paper mediates. The early and mid-Victorian *Times* is the best known case. Similarly the rise of the *Manchester Guardian* at the end of the nineteenth century was closely associated with the social groups who were asserting their claim to 'responsibilty' through the Liberal Party. More recently circulation increases in the daily and Sunday 'qualities' testify not simply to the spread of higher education within the middle class (and to a smaller extent, its increased penetration amongst the working class) but to the increased *political* relevance of education. An advanced industrial economy needs highly-trained specialists at many levels. The (late) political recognition of this was interestingly prefigured in the social prestige which some advertising stereotypes began to confer on education in the fifties. (The old anti-highbrow appeal has almost disappeared.) The very advertising campaigns of 'quality' newspapers address themselves to 'bright lively minds', 'top people' (i.e. non-top people pursuing the career of the talents). In the Meritocracy, 'responsible' readers are all educated. Even the *Daily Mail* now looks out for 'busy *thinkers*'.

Nor is this just a matter of external catchwords. A commonplace of the economics of today's serious newspaper is the degree of its dependence on advertising revenue. (The 1962 Royal Commission calculated that in 1960, for national morning papers the proportion of income from sales and from advertising was 25 per cent and 75 per cent respectively for 'qualities', and 45 per cent and 55 per cent for 'populars'; for national Sundays the proportions were 21 per cent and 79 per cent as against 51 per cent and 49 per cent.) And this dependence is more than economic. Modern advertising works by manipulating various symbols so as to confer social prestige on the things it tries to sell. These symbols are very largely drawn from the language of class-discrimination. Clearly, the readers of the 'quality' Press, no less than the readers of the 'populars', respond to this language, otherwise the advertisers would find another. The claim of the *Sunday Express* to be, with the *Observer*, the *Sunday Times*, and the *Sunday Telegraph*, a 'quality' paper throws a usefully harsh light on the ambiguity of this term. Why do 'responsible' readers react to such advertising? Because one way of associating yourself with government is by acquiring a life-style symbolically associated with older 'responsible' classes. (See the interplay of appeals to 'tradition' and 'modernity' in the advertising for furniture.) The advertising in the serious Press helps to provide the emotional education which its readers require for their (partly fictional) 'responsible' role. It further provides emotional consolation for the consciousness that this role *is* partly fictional, and there is a link here with the advertising in some 'populars' where the rhetoric of compensation is brasher and shriller – more obviously compensatory, in fact. If advertising in the serious Press is much more prominent than fifty years ago, then that is partly because earlier serious newspapers could depend on their 'responsible' readers being subject to useful rhetorics elsewhere; from the pulpit, or in much literature. Tennyson, one of the masters of Victorian social rhetoric, rose to the peak of his fame during the decade in which Delane wrote his famous editorial.

To say this is not to depreciate the intellectual and moral values which ideally, and to some extent in practice, the serious Press embodies. But to forget it is to subscribe to the notion that these values exist in a political and social vacuum. The tone of the serious Press often suggests that it grossly overrates its own detachment from the social-political context within which it operates. This position leads also to a serious failure to understand the 'emotionalism' of the 'popular' Press, or to conceive of any real alternative to the present state of affairs. The more complex picture of the serious Press and its readers also makes sense of certain recent developments, not conformable to the traditional ideal. There is the magazine tendency where, as in an earlier phase of 'popular' journalism, the varied contents of the Sunday papers have been imitated in the comparable dailies: articles on fashion, books, science, travel, cultural, and hobby pursuits interleaved with the customary political fare. Why have these subjects migrated from their own specialist journals (losing, it should be added, much of their indigenous plumage on the way)? If we think of the serious Press as ritualizing a way of life as well as fulfilling a political role, heterogeneity of content is only to be expected. The magazine tendency as a whole merges with the advertising in its role of emotional confirmation, and in answering the reader's search for identity. In fact, as has often been pointed out, there is sometimes little to choose between advertisements and feature articles. Another recent development, reinforced by the magazine tendency if not actually part of it, is the multiplication of feature articles on political subjects, of personalized reporting, and interpretation intended to do the reader's thinking for him in an idiom which for various reasons he finds satisfying. On their own, facts have to be understood and interpreted; and leader arguments are in a tradition and language which invite conscious assent or disagreement. But the reassuring caption 'From Our Industrial Correspondent' lulls the energies invoked by straight reporting and straight commentary, and half-authorizes selective reporting and unargued views. (A recent example of this was the *Guardian*'s front-page reporting of the unilateralist debate in the Labour Party in 1960, which was, unwittingly one presumes, pro-Gaitskell – the position it was arguing in its own comments.) This is not necessarily a bad thing despite its undermining of the traditional dogma: styles and conventions develop with all genuine communication, and many topics gain from a condensed, and so selective, presentation. But it is worth being clear about it: the 'responsible' reader takes a great deal on trust; he likes the world to be presented to him in a certain way; even the political relationship between him and his paper has its rituals. Serious political papers are usually classified in terms of express political affiliation. An equally, if not more illuminating description would emerge from a study of the different rituals with which they familiarize the world for their readers. It would lead at least to a less rationalistic account of the Press as a whole.

3

What distinguishes the serious Press, filling with varied success the political role, from other newspapers? The latter will usually point to their larger circulations; the advertiser will underline contrasts in the wealth of the readerships; the serious Press itself could divide the remainder into two groups: those attempting the political role in an illegitimate spirit, and those that largely ignore it. Both latter types have, in fact, much in common: notably a primary interest in money-making, and a shared method of attaining it.

In a classic denunciation of the Press in its illegitimate political role, Stanley Baldwin described two papers, Beaverbrook's *Daily Express* and Rothermere's *Daily Mail*, in these terms: '... not newspapers in the ordinary acceptation of the term ...' but '... engines of propaganda for the constantly changing policies, desires, personal wishes, personal likes and dislikes of [their owners]'; employing methods of '... direct falsehood, misrepresentation, half-truths ... suppression and editorial criticism of speeches which are not reported ...' in the furtherance of the owners' aims. The two Lords had been trying to exert direct political pressure on Baldwin's position within his own party. Baldwin's criticism usefully underlines the link between their pursuit of direct political power and the newspapers' defiance of the rules which characterize the legitimate political role. The procedure he describes permits an editor to mould reality into a shape suitably docile to the propaganda of the owner whom he serves. What, formally, such a newspaper offers as 'facts' are in truth arguments in disguise 'proving' the arguments that are explicit. It is as necessary to preserve the *formula* of true-facts-distinct-from-free-comment – simple advocacy is less effective, and not what people buy newspapers for – as it is to destroy the substance, the real tension between commentary and report which always guarantees the good faith of a newspaper. But the moulding of reality need not take this extreme form. There are subtler methods, harder to controvert because no longer aiming at direct power, but having political effect not less important because indirect. This effect stems less from the espousing of views – a vendetta against the British Council, or the United Nations – as from the picture of the world which selection and emphasis rather than downright untruth builds up in the reports. When this is created primarily for its psychological effect on the reader, it supports not so much a particular range of formulated opinions as the less-consciously held attitudes from which opinions emerge; and most notably, the kind of relationship which the reader feels himself to have with the reported world. In practice, this means two things: sensationalism and triviality. Important political events are treated as sources of fear, excitement, exultation, alarm; or curiosity, 'human interest', 'warmth'. Other events – disaster, gossip, domestic incidents, crimes, 'tit-bits' – are offered as of equal interest with the political events. Typographical devices intertwine the sets of occurrences: headlining, position on page, photographs. From whatever source, each event is presented in terms of some attitude which the reader will find it emotionally satisfying to adopt. (There is a certain analogy here with some personalized reporting in the serious Press, but contrast the deliberately comic headlining that can occur in *The Times*.) Like salesmen with a difficult product, these newspapers concentrate all their energy on the emotional make-up of their readers. This may seem (so certainly it is claimed) to offer a more generous attitude towards people than the 'dull rationalism' of the serious Press – a defence that would be more convincing if it were less obviously self-interested. It is more plausibly maintained that all reporting, page-making, and sub-editing, that the very process of communication in any medium, involves selection and emphasis, and that the 'popular' presentation of the world in some large circulation dailies is no more than a style among others, chosen in relation to a particular audience. This is to an extent true: the serious Press has its own varied conventions and procedures which can be seen to correspond to different groups of 'responsible' readers. But the difference lies in the spirit in which each 'style' is set to work. No newspaper can present an objective world, but the scrupulous ones, recognizing this, say in effect: 'though this is how the world seems to me today, my own values necessarily enter into the presentation.' The unscrupulous paper says: 'this is a true picture of the world – ignore other versions as false, irrelevant, or boring.' Nothing is easier than to couple this message, daily dramatized in the whole typographical and verbal structure of the paper, with hearty declarations about freedom of comment. Unrelated to a world of events in which both reader and opinion have a significant role, this freedom is meaningless, 'free' only to act as another source of psychological gratification. In this context, opinions are never 'relevant', 'convincing', 'well or badly supported', but 'fearless', 'provocative', 'challenging', which, having nothing to do with *action,* they can well afford to be.

The real key to the political influence of such papers lies neither in the opinions which they propagate, nor in the attitudes which, in their preoccupation with 'human interest', they endorse or actively feed. It lies in the implication that without their colourful intervention there is no meaningful relationship between the events which they dramatize and the readers for whom the show goes on. In this respect, their 'style' has a hidden content. It speaks for readers whom it takes to be politically disenfranchised, for whom the news of political events is not about a world in which they feel they can meaningfully act. This is the more subtle form of political manipulation since it imposes on the reader an assumption of which he remains unaware. It also makes it easier to speak on his behalf. It is, in sum, the modern way of 'forming and supplying the opinions of the people'.

Between the illegitimate politics of the 'populars' and the newspaper whose primary function is to 'entertain', there are certain differences. If the political manipulator entertains, this is always less for its own sake than as a tacit bribe to the reader for allowing himself now and again to be violently jerked in a definite political direction. But when 'entertainment' (i.e. profit) is the goal, political material is both reduced in quantity, and subordinate in place. Typographical devices often submerge what there is into other material; or separate it off altogether from the major interests of sport, gossip, and crime (e.g. the *Mirror*'s feature, 'World News Spotlight' – significant metaphor). In the tabloid presentation, 'entertainment' assimilates everything into a fictional melodrama. Symbolized in the paper's 'personality', the reader becomes the hero of an endless tale, subjecting the world of 'them' (i.e. everything which the rhetoric cannot reduce) to magical defeats and rejections. What the defenders of the tabloid manner seem incapable of understanding is that theirs is not 'just a way of putting it' – a real victory for the newspaper's political role under unrewarding circumstances. (cf. Arnold's remark at the head of this chapter, and see the moving story told by Collins and King in the record of the NUT conference.) Whatever the nobly-educative intentions of the speaker, if *this* is his idiom then the effective content of his message shrinks and coarsens accordingly. Few issues, at any level, can survive this. Is it not better in this situation to abandon the pretence at anything resembling the political role, and admit to the guiding assumption that the audience in question finds the world of serious politics meaningless because it has no direct *continuous* participation? In effect, of course, precisely this admission gets made when apologists answer critics by denying the relevance of daily political reporting 'uplift' to this audience. On the other hand, with issues that engage the direct interest of the owner (like the Pilkington Report) the 'tabloid' handling becomes indistinguishable from that of the political manipulator.

For different reasons then, or with different emphases, both categories of newspaper look on their readers as 'irresponsible' – open to manipulation, looking mainly to be amused, not intelligently related to the reported world, as politically disenfranchised.* Before proceeding then to the customary denunciation, it seems worth while asking whether there is not a very substantial social and political reality which partly justifies this assumption. Like the serious newspapers, the 'popular'

* The social distribution of the different categories shows that readers like this are widely diffused through the whole society. (See *The Long Revolution*, pp. 211–13.) One of the strong motives such papers play on is the temptation we all share to lapse into effective disenfranchisement, to accept a passive role. In this, of course, they cooperate with tendencies in the political structure.

and 'tabloid' function within a whole cultural context. If they represent something of what 'the public wants', there are likely to be good reasons for the public's taste ; reasons beyond the common interest in the immediately striking, in the superficial, in the melodramatic. There is fiction in the assumption of the serious Press that its readers are wholly 'responsible' about what they read – able to interpret, ready to act. There is a corresponding reality in the assumptions of the large-circulation dailies. Seen in this light, we can explain the 'popular' presentation of serious politics as one result of the gap between the political forms and the political reality. That politics is treated at all corresponds to the theoretical expectations of a democratic structure. The treatment it actually gets – the myth-making, the idiom which calls every difference of opinion a 'row', and turns every issue into 'personal' terms, the sloganized parody that passes for debate, the daily processing* of political experience – all these show the reality. For this state of affairs, the responsibility of the newspaper owners is certainly great. Their barbarian misuse of these profoundly needed social institutions is still one of the scandals of our century. Nevertheless, any major change in these 'communication' styles necessarily implies equally major changes in the relationship which readers both have and feel themselves to have towards the world of decision and government. This awkward truth cannot be by-passed by grumbling about the stupidity and laziness of the readers of the large-circulation dailies. The numbers of people involved are simply too large for judgements like that

* A. R. Crosland thinks use of the term *processing* betrays deep intellectual snobbery. (See his 'The Mass Media' in *Encounter*, November 1962.) So I had better explain my own, and indeed what I take to be the usual meaning. *Processing* means re-stating something within a set of conventions which transfer interest from the thing transmitted to the experience of transmission. Mr Crosland draws an astounding analogy between teaching and 'popular' styles of transmission: each involves simplification and dilution, he says, each is a kind of 'processing'. But there is this difference: a teacher aims to build a relationship between his subject matter and his pupils *independent of himself*, while mass media 'processing' imposes upon *all* subject-matters a prior relationship between medium and audience. The nature of this relationship is such as to reduce most subject-matters. Needless to say, not all mass-media transmission is 'processing'.

to have any meaning; and the individuals who make up these numbers are, in other areas of their experience, capable, and sane. A main accusation against the purveyors of the large circulation dailies is certainly that they build and maintain a major barrier to change and growth – for without the fuller and more continuous participation in the processes of government by real (and not formal) majorities of people this growth will not come. But in this accusation must be included the submerged assumptions of a good deal of 'responsible' criticism of their products.

It remains to say something explicit about 'entertainment' as such, since the attack on this from 'responsible' quarters is sometimes misconceived. All contemporary newspapers 'entertain', and in doing so follow a tradition as old as the more celebrated political role. Coleridge, who has been quoted in connexion with the political role, himself contributed serious journalism on contemporary affairs when he wrote for the *Morning Post*. Yet it was the same paper which published his (amongst others') poems, claiming that some relief was due to its readers from 'ferocious politics'. Again, in the Victorian period, 'entertaining' Sunday papers largely devoted to crime-reporting achieved very large circulations. Northcliffe's 'revolution', seen not in its crucial economic aspect, but stylistically, was an adaptation of the human-interest of these Victorian Sundays for the new daily audience. In our century, the new development has been, in some quarters, the dissolution of the old barrier between politics and other material, so that, in the words of the song, 'The world is a show,/ The show is a world/ Of entertainment.' Most recently, the spread of 'entertainment' into the serious dailies has made it more difficult to see that lure alone as the fault of 'populars' and 'tabloids'. But what, exactly, is 'entertainment' in its modern sense? As far as the Press goes (and even further – the areas colonized by much television, most magazines, many films), its main function can be described as one of attitude-propping. At many levels, 'entertainment' supplies a cultural and moral rhetoric, an easy confirmation of group-feeling, a temporary but repeated answer to the demand for reassurance and approval. Despite the appearance of abundance and variety, 'entertainment' turns out to be remarkably uniform. For a given audience, sport, fashion, intellectual and cultural news, fantasy, gossip, disguised gossip – chatty surveys of complex social phenomena – are all rendered in a common idiom, whose aim is to reassure the reader that all these matters are easily accessible, or reducible, within his scheme of values. Like a drug, this is, at any level, both addictive and enervating, and in particular cases (book reviewing is probably the best known) becomes more satisfying than the material it reduces. Like the selling of political news in 'human interest' and other wrappers, 'entertainment' reveals a deep nervousness about the unaided relevance and value of what it is dealing with. There is a constant tendency to humorous and witty treatment, of the imposition of a reducing tone of voice. The diffusion of this through the media is perhaps the most striking demonstration of the essential unity of function of 'entertainment' at all levels, in every context. See, for example, the radio survey of political opinion in the weeklies on Saturday mornings; or the way 'Woman's Hour' presents incidents from ordinary life in extraordinary stylized scripts – the 'ordinary' people read these and the gap between the real human voice and the idiom imposed by the script is painful; visually, there is the stylized head-jerking of most television commentators, e.g. the 'Tonight' team and the bland emollience of the central commentator in weekly discussion programmes; or the synthetic chauvinism of the sports commentators exciting themselves about Britain's prospect of 'a gold'.

What this indicates is a much closer relation between the 'popular' and 'serious' Press than their different handlings of political material would suggest. The 'homely' personality of the tabloid paper, and to a lesser extent but with other additions, of the 'popular' daily, derives primarily from a need for a large amorphous undifferentiated audience. It must be large, because its individual members are not especially rich, and the advertising rates it can command not high. The existence of an audience like this depends on a fictional sense of identity provided in the style of the paper. Only a national diffusion of the audience will ensure a large enough sale, and this has to be created by excluding the differentiae of the regional and other minority groups which compose this audience. 'Entertainment' plays the key part in maintaining the fiction. It evokes from any given subject matter the particular range of attitudes which make up the paper's personality. Features contribute a great deal to this process. ('In the *Mirror* the letters to the Editor get up to fifty-nine per cent [of the readership]' reports John Beavan in *The Press & The Public*, Fabian Tract 338 (1962). These letters are evidently picked for their display of 'attitude'. The next highest percentage, fifty-eight per cent, is for sport.) This same close connexion between newspaper-economics and entertainment-style exists in the serious Press, especially the Sundays, where again the advertising revenue depends on keeping readers with a certain income. To hold this audience the relevant 'attitude-propping' develops both in the formal contents – tone of voice, and range of topics – and in advertising style. (A simple illustration is from the *New Statesman*, which holds a competition for the 'best' advertisement to appear in its pages. The prize exhibits strikingly mimic the standard tone of the *reviewing* columns. The judge of the competition is V. S. Pritchett, one of its veteran literary contributors.)

It is easier to describe than to make any general assessment of 'entertainment', and of the magazine influence. Defenders can always claim that newspapers are now more varied; critics that this, precisely, is what is wrong. Clearly, there are good things – which would at the 'popular' level especially be better if they were not styled and shaped by rigid conventions – and there is a great deal of the trivial and boring, at every level. Two points, however, widely apply. The source of feature writing is very often specialist books and journals – 'entertainment' feeds on these too often parasitically, returning nothing to the stock of original knowledge and work on which its own life depends. The serious Press might well consider subsidizing or contributing to specialist periodicals instead of continuously expanding their review pages and multiplying their feature articles. At the same time, they might set a general example as to tone by discouraging the baseless judicial pretensions of the people who do the feature writing. Is it too much to hope that 'entertainment' might make more use of the simple unopinionated report (not that there is anything simple about reporting)? But even if it did, the reader's thirst for social magic, spelling out the imaginary group-identities, would no doubt remain. With 'entertainment' above all, the larger social context has its relevance.

4

Concrete proposals for the reform of the contemporary Press fall into two categories: educational procedures, and institutional changes. The educationist hopes that if enough people learn to read a newspaper critically, the owners will have to change their ways. He would like to make the critical assessment of newspaper-contents a regular part of general education, and one of the lettered skills which the G.C.E. recognizes and tests. Valuable work has for some years been done on these lines, and the new liberal arts courses for students at technical colleges, the day-release courses and the teacher's training certificate offer scope for its extension. Analysis like this need not be confined to newspapers only, but can link with discussions of television and film in one way, and with literature and art in another. There is, though, one problem about these schemes: the skills in question cannot be taught as mere skills. They involve complex processes of judgement which can only be truly exercised by direct experience of another kind of communication than that practised in the national dailies. How, within the educational structure, can this be achieved? It seems reasonable to ask whether, with the best will and the finest training, the teacher/pupil relationship with its own necessary conventions and perspective is an altogether adequate model. Fuller, more flexible practice in communication might arise from the actual use of the media by the pupils – newspaper, television, radio, and film – not for 'educational purposes', but for the direct exploration and interchange of their own experience of their own world. The comparative study of different reports of the same event would benefit if the event fell within the range of the child's (preferably passionate) experiences and interests. It would provide a more dramatic and telling illustration of the relativity of all reporting than any material to be found in a newspaper. It is this fact that makes tentativeness and good faith so crucial in all human communication, and the bad faith of the contemporary newspaper practice would be more meaningful. How real, even to a sixteen-year-old child, is the world which his study of the Press will lead him to suspect? For all but the bright students (whose other studies will in any case equip them with some of the relevant skills) is the material of the Press near enough to direct experience to yield the freshness of response without which the most compelling analysis of value is useless? The same arguments hold, in fact, for the study of newspapers as for literature: more writing and less discussion. The problems of page-making, the effect of different headlines, reporting in different styles and from different premises would all be natural developments from a school newspaper working within the educational structure (and not, of course, used as a prestige bulletin, or for the handing down of adult guidance). The mechanics of printing would give direct knowledge of the influence wielded by technical factors. Large comprehensive schools would gain in real identity by possessing such a medium for inter-communication between the various age-groups and specialisms. There are obvious dangers but if the main goal is kept in mind – that communication should become a 'natural' part of human life – none that could not be surmounted. The critical counter-pressure that could develop against the contemporary 'popular' Press would not only be armed with analytic weapons, but propelled by a substantially different assumption about the use of language.

The other category of reforms concerns the structure of the Press itself, and the possibility of building institutional checks and safeguards against the more familiar shortcomings: pressure from advertisers, unscrupulous behaviour by journalists, inaccuracies, and sensationalism. Currently, the immediate need is to adopt the recommendation of the 1949 Royal Commission that the Press Council should include a number of lay members. The 1962 Commission has repeated this proposal.* Despite some good work, the Council has repeatedly failed to show that its professional ethic is adequate to the tasks of effective self-criticism. A professional group can only claim to regulate its own social responsibility if it acts upon standards which satisfy the lay public (e.g. medicine, and law). Sir Norman Angell proposed the setting up of a panel of highly experienced journalists who would write and edit a special newspaper, maintaining the most scrupulous standards in relation to facts, alleged facts, inferences from facts, and rumours. Such a publication might not be widely read, and would have to be subsidized, but it would act as a standard, with a general bracing effect. Other suggestions are the compulsory correction of mistakes (with fines for failure) in prominent type and place; and compulsory space for the views of opponents to the paper's general policy. But all these proposals, and especially the latter group, fail to touch the inner problem of the 'popular' and 'tabloid' Press. There can never be laws against 'entertainment'. The standards of the serious Press at its best only become relevant if there is felt relationship between the reader and the news he is offered. This relationship cannot be created by adjustments within the current structure, dominated as it is by the newspaper owners from whose imperatives so many of the difficulties flow. The key to the problem lies in the economic and not in the institutional structure. As long as a major section of the Press can be treated as a commodity, primarily subject like other market products to the demand for profitable returns on the heavy capital investment needed by the modern printing industry, there is little room for movement except along the road which the Press is now travelling: mergers, concentration of resources in fewer and fewer hands, homogeneity in the product plus marginal differentiation (like the soap powders). The serious Press can resist to an extent (though as its magazine-tendency shows much less powerfully than it imagines) because of the greater advertising revenues it can command. Political traditions outside the Press are at present saving the *Daily Herald* from the pressures to which the *News Chronicle* succumbed

*Which has now been put into practice.

(aided, however, by internal failures of its own). But it is not likely to survive beyond the time-limit, unless it can compete with the *Daily Mirror*, which seems unlikely.* Change of another kind can only come from another source: the Press has no way of resisting or checking the energy of its own dynamic. This indeed, is one of the depressing aspects of the current scene; the needed major criticisms do not come from within the profession.

There is no space here to develop the full argument for other kinds of proposal, but a sketch may indicate a more fruitful line of thinking. The search for profit leads to the Press's major dependence on advertising, and this in its turn dominates the style and content of what is published. If it were not for the artificially created national 'popular' audience, the conventions of 'entertainment' could be less strict, the need to 'sell' the news less pressing, the possibility of a genuine relationship between paper and readers more likely. The circulation of the national dailies was built up by destroying a flourishing independent local Press. Is it possible to reverse this process? Not in any simple way, of course, but the model is a valuable guide. If we had instead of one or two papers with a 3–4 million circulation, six or seven with a circulation of about 900,000–1,000,000 based largely on the major regions of the country, the 'popular' Press would present a much less depressing sight. One of the powerful impulses which the conventions of the national Press mobilize is the need for group-identities. (cf. the use made of regional voices on radio and television for their 'warmth' and 'popular' quality.) A reconstructed Press could find in this a more genuine tone which, far from being parochial, would be the right medium for communicating between the local and regional audience and the national and international scene. The only national dailies that are really *needed* are those which communicate news in which readers genuinely participate as members of the larger community. One would, in fact, hope to see the assimilation of the 'serious' Press to such dailies, or alternatively, a cut-down and amalgamated serious Press for professionals and specialists – subsidized if necessary.

*It is now known that the *Daily Herald* will not survive beyond 1964.

There is only one way in which this could come about: a decision to subsidize from public funds for a substantial period, perhaps ten years, the costs of printing and distributing at least two new papers, regionally based. These would not be 'official' sheets, but be run by practising journalists in an initially exploratory spirit, building perhaps from a surviving local weekly, a genuine paper of its community.* They would compete with the national dailies by providing much more truly 'what the public wants', because they would be in a position to take this more seriously than the 'popular' Press does. The aim would be to reduce the circulation of national dailies by offering readers a genuine identity, instead of the bullying rhetoric of the current fiction. They would not, one hopes, set out to be regional 'qualities', but more like regional 'populars' released from the exigencies of owner's politics *and* profits. They could be much more miscellaneous, less uniform in tone and manner. They could develop natural connexions with local school newspapers which would provide continuity for each. They would, if successful, begin to attract advertising from the national dailies, the effect of which could only be to raise the prices of the latter, and so, eventually depress their circulations. If this pressure were maintained, the nationals would have to adjust to the different sort of audience which was being created. At the end of ten years, the position could be surveyed with a view to seeing whether decreasing the subsidy and raising the price would enable them to continue on a more permanent basis.

There seems to be no other way of breaking the hegemony of the advertising revenue but by this deliberate creation of a real alternative to it. In the long run, no change could, of course, be permanent without major assistance from the educational structure, or major changes in the degree of participation in government. But such changes could not come about by educational pressure alone, because in this field a main 'educational' force is the current situation, and not the formal training given in schools. One need not, of course, underrate the opposition that other than educational proposals would arouse.

*cf. the current argument for the protection and development of regional economies by the central government.

DISCRIMINATION AND POPULAR CULTURE

'... it is necessary to break through to the central fact that most of our cultural institutions are in the hands of speculators, interested not in the health and growth of the society, but in the quick profits that can be made by exploiting inexperience.' (*The Long Revolution* p. 338.) To appeal from profit to the health of the society has never been a simple matter, but the longer the appeal is delayed the more difficult it becomes to formulate, the vaguer and stranger to the imagination the values it depends on. The speculation, meanwhile, will go on.

*

BOOKS

NORMAN ANGELL, *The Press & The Organisation of Society* (Heffer, 1932)

KINGSLEY MARTIN, *The Press The Public Wants* (1947)

FRANCIS WILLIAMS, *Dangerous Estate* (Longmans, 1955)

RICHARD HOGGART, 'Mass Communications in Britain' in *The Modern Age,* ed. B. Ford (Pelican, 1961)

BRIAN GROOMBRIDGE, *Popular Culture and Personal Responsibility: A Study Outline* (NUT, 1961)

RAYMOND WILLIAMS, *Communications* (Penguin, 1962)

5   The Film

ALBERT HUNT

People like Mr Anderson perform a valuable service when they draw attention to hidden significances and covert propaganda, but the normal person will go on regarding the screen with the unseeing gaze Watson fixed on his bowler – and perhaps be none the worse for it.
The Times

Too much high-flown nonsense is talked about art and culture in relation to films.

MISS C. A. LEJEUNE (Film Critic)

Last night to the flicks. All war films. One very good one of a ship full of refugees being bombed somewhere in the Mediterranean. Audience much amused by shots of a great huge fat man trying to swim away with a helicopter after him, first you saw him wallowing in the water like a porpoise, then you saw him through the helicopter's gunsights, then he was full of holes and the sea round him turned pink and he sank as suddenly as though the holes had let in the water. audience shouting with laughter as he sank. then you saw a lifeboat full of children with a helicopter hovering over it. there was a middle-aged woman ... sitting up in the bow with a little boy about three years old in her arms. little boy screaming with fright and hiding his head between her breasts as if he was trying to burrow right into her and the woman putting her arms round him ... all the time covering him up ... as if she thought her arms could keep the bullets off. then the helicopter planted a 20 kilo bomb in among them ... then there was a wonderful shot of a child's arm going up up up right up into the air a helicopter with a camera in its nose must have followed it up and there was a lot of applause from the party seats. ...

GEORGE ORWELL: *Nineteen Eighty-Four*

The cinema is the most important of all the arts.

LENIN

1

Although in recent years cinema-going has declined, the film clearly remains one of the most important of the new means of communication. There are a number of reasons for this.

In the first place, the influence of the film is still very wide-spread. The coming of television has led to a crisis in the industry and to the closing of a lot of cinemas. But against this must be set the increasing use of film material on television itself. The circumstances of viewing have changed, but television has made the film a part of our everyday life. There must be very few people who pass through any week in this country without coming into contact with a film of some kind.

Secondly, the film is distinct from the rest of the new media in that so far it is the only one to have developed into an art form. In the sixty or so years of its existence, the film has not reached the maturity of the Shakespearian theatre or of the best nineteenth-century novels; but films like Buñuel's *L'Age d'Or*, Vigo's *L'Atalante* and Renoir's *La Règle du Jeu* will bear comparison with most twentieth-century art. In the case of the film, modern technology has made possible a genuine extension of aesthetic experience.

Thirdly, the directness and immediacy of the film have made this experience accessible to a very wide audience. This is not to suggest that all films are easy to understand, or that most film-goers would like *L'Atalante*. But the gap between the good and the popular has been less fixed in the cinema than in the more traditional art forms. Film-makers like Chaplin, Hitch-cock, John Ford, and Howard Hawks have shown that it is possible to use such popular forms as the slapstick comedy, the thriller, and the western in an intelligent and adult way. And a film as seriously intentioned as *Saturday Night and Sunday Morning* can still be one of the most popular films of the year.

The film, however, is not only an art form. Like the rest of the media, it is a major industry. In 1905, a seven-minute British film, *Rescued by Rover*, was made for £7 13s. 9d. The modern three-hour epic, which is the industry's principal answer to television, costs about two million pounds, and the average cost of an ordinary feature film made in British or American studios is £150,000.

Any art which demands capital investment on such a scale inevitably becomes involved with the industrial trends of modern society. There has been a tendency towards centralization, and control has come to rest in a very few hands. In Britain, for example, film distribution is virtually dependent on two companies which run the circuit cinemas, and since films can normally be financed only on guarantees of distribution, this means that two companies have almost complete control over what films are to be made, and what subjects are acceptable.

What is the effect of this situation on an important art form? How are those who control the film industry using this powerful medium? And how does this matter to those of us who care about our culture?

The answers to these questions seem to me to be particularly urgent in any consideration of popular culture today.

2

The films we normally think of in connexion with the film industry come into the category of entertainment. As such, they have been generally ignored by people concerned with education. Typical of an attitude that is widely held is the evidence submitted to Pilkington by the National Broadcasting Development Committee, which includes the following statement:

There are people who argue that ... television ... should be devoted much more obviously to the task of educating the public in the moral, social, and cultural values of our civilization. We would state most emphatically that this is one of the functions ... television should perform in this country. However, it is indeed naïve to believe that a ... programme ... could be successful if it did not contain a large measure of pure entertainment.

The Committee's evidence refers to television, but the

101

assumption behind it is directly related to any discussion of the entertainment film. For the statement assumes that, on the one hand, we have the 'values of our civilization', which are established and never-changing; and on the other we have 'pure entertainment', which in no way affects them.

This assumption needs, I believe, to be carefully examined. What does the film industry offer us as 'pure entertainment'? Is there no connexion between the offerings and our 'moral, social, and cultural values'?

It is tempting to answer these questions in general terms. The guardians of our cultural standards have often directed a lot of accusations against the cinema, and some of them have been extravagant and hysterical, and based on a complete lack of information. 'No, I have not seen *Rocco*,' a correspondent in the *Guardian* wrote of a distinguished Italian film, 'and I don't suppose I shall'; but this didn't prevent him from condemning the film as depraved on the strength of newspaper accounts of a sequence the censor had removed.

Such general accusations merely confuse the issue. Before we can begin to make any useful comments, we need to come to terms with the precise way in which a film communicates – with the movements, gestures, compositions, and sounds which together make up the language of the film.

A film is, basically, an arrangement of moving pictures and recorded sounds. The man responsible for this arrangement is the director. It is his job to select what the camera is going to record, and to organize it into film shape.

The director has at his disposal a wide range of possibilities, from close-up to long shot, from placing the camera at a low angle to shooting from high above the action, from holding the camera still and allowing the movements inside the frame to speak for themselves, to moving it freely in any direction, coming in close to isolate a particular feature, or drawing back to set it in perspective. The film is, in the end, the sum of the director's choices.

Each of these possibilities contributes to the way a film communicates. When D. W. Griffith composed his close-up of a pair of hands at the climax of the trial in *Intolerance*, he demonstrated a particular way of communicating physical tension. And when Hitchcock, in *Psycho*, shows us a pair of frightened eyes, staring at us through driving rain from behind the hypnotically swinging windscreen-wipers of a car, he presents us with a concrete image of the unease that lies below the surface of the everyday world.

It is through his choices that a director reveals his way of thinking and feeling. In *Paths of Glory*, for example, a film about the First World War, Stanley Kubrick makes the quick cut from one scene to another a part of the fabric of his conception of the war: he sets side by side the misery of the men in the trenches and the luxury of the château behind the front line where the generals plan the next battle. By contrast, the Italian director, De Sica, in *Umberto D*, uses an almost motionless camera to communicate his sense of the importance and mysteriousness of the most habitual actions: he lets his camera rest for several minutes on a servant-girl grinding coffee, so that her every movement becomes interesting and strange.

If the director's response to what he experiences is crude and conventional – or if he thinks of films as junk for the masses – the crudity and lack of conviction will be reflected in the style of his film. But in the hands of a serious artist, the simplest elements of film-making can bear the weight of a complex poetic statement.

For example, in Franju's short film, *Hôtel des Invalides*, there is a shot of the courtyard of victory in the Paris war museum. The picture is geometrical in its composition. A building is all rectangular lines, cannons are arranged in regular patterns, the branches of trees are clipped, straight, and bare. The only movement in the picture comes from a leaf in the foreground which sways gently backwards and forwards in the breeze. On the sound-track, we hear the twittering of birds.

It is difficult to translate the effect of this image into words. There is the sterility of conquest, the hollowness of military glory, the menacing and destructive rigidity of organized war. But Franju also reminds us of the fragile spontaneity that the war machine has almost, but not quite, crushed; and of the indifference of the leaf and the birds to the grandiose patterns of military honour.

To create this complexity of feeling, Franju has gone right back to the origins of cinema. 'Look, the leaves are moving!' cried somebody in one of the first audiences ever to be confronted with a moving picture. Franju has taken a moving leaf, and has used it as one of the elements in an image that has all the economy and imaginative force of true art.

3

The film, then, is the concrete expression of the director's imagination. It is only by exploring the form of that expression that we can hope to make any valid judgements about film. But if we turn from *Hôtel des Invalides* and examine, in this way, some of the typical products of the film industry, we shall be in a position to understand much more clearly the nature of the links between 'pure entertainment' and the 'values of our civilization'.

These links, together with the effects of the economic pressures inside the film industry, can, perhaps, be most clearly shown by a brief analysis of three fairly recent British productions. The first two, *The Guns of Navarone* and *The Young Ones*, have both been box-office successes in Britain in the last few years, particularly with young people. The third, *The Angry Silence*, was made about five years ago by a new independent company, and was welcomed as an example of a more enlightened attitude in the industry. (In selecting these films, I am aware that I am laying myself open to the charge of rigging the evidence; but most people would, I think, agree that they are typical and are, if anything, better than average productions.)

The Guns of Navarone is about an episode in the last war. It is one of a series of British films describing war adventures – they appear less frequently now than they did a few years ago, but the success of this particular film suggests that the vogue is far from over. The film is directed by J. Lee Thompson, a technically skilful director, who has made many films of this kind, and has the benefit of a script by the American, Carl Foreman, who is well known for his unusually intelligent scripting of a western, *High Noon*.

The film tells the story of a commando expedition sent to silence two German guns on the island of Navarone in the Greek archipelago. The guns command a narrow strip of water through which men from another island have to be evacuated. There is plenty of physical excitement, including the destruction of an E-boat, a storm, and a ship-wreck, a climb up an almost impassable cliff, a capture and an escape in enemy uniform, the unmasking of a traitor, and finally in a race against time, the spectacular destruction of the guns. It is what is sometimes described as a healthy schoolboy yarn.

But if we stop to examine what the film is communicating, through its form of expression, a number of important assumptions begin to emerge.

The film opens with a prologue, which is accompanied by a portentous commentary. Set into the large screen, with its picturesque colour film of the Greek islands, are black and white newsreels of the Mediterranean campaign. The effect of this is to establish a link with reality – with a real war about real issues in which real people were killed. The documentary link is kept by the device of introducing each part of the story with a log-book title such as, 'First Day – 0.600 hours'.

Moreover, Foreman's dialogue raises several moral problems. A conversation between two officers approaches the basic dilemma of fighting a modern total war – to win, you have to become as nasty as the thing you're fighting. 'Bearing in mind that we're on the side of decency and civilization,' says the officer in command, played by Gregory Peck, 'would you say that was a civilized thing to do?' He has just told another wounded officer a lie, so that under torture he will still be useful in giving false information. And there is a corporal, played by David Niven, who refuses to become an officer because he doesn't want to be responsible for the dirty work of killing; while another man, known as 'the butcher of Barcelona', who has been killing Germans since 1937, says that he now finds the job distasteful. These problems are all clearly and directly related to the 'values of our civilization': and so is the way they are treated.

Consider, for instance, the moment when the corporal discovers that he *is* responsible, that he has to take his share of the moral responsibility. He is laying the fuse to blow up the guns, and he suddenly says, 'I'm up to my neck in it, aren't I?' – and the camera shows him standing in a hole with only his head from the neck upwards visible. It isn't only that a serious moral issue is turned, by the scripting and the placing of the camera, into a joke. The trouble is that the joke is so feeble and trite.

Or consider the scene in which the men discover that one of the Greek girls has betrayed them. The girl claims to have scars on her back that have been inflicted by the Germans. The claim is proved false when her dress is ripped off her shoulders to reveal smooth white flesh. As the officers discuss the morality of shooting her, she is shown lying on the floor and weeping, the front of her dress clutched to her almost visible breasts. What makes the scene so dreary is the sheer glumness of it all; the director goes out of his way to give us a peep at a pretty body – but while peeping we're expected to pretend that all we're interested in is a moral problem.

Again, a man with gangrene in his leg is tortured. A Nazi officer stands over him, moving the splints with the butt of a revolver. He is young, blond, and blue-eyed, with an ice-cold mask of a face (it is worth noting, incidentally, that we are here being invited to adopt the Nazi practice of hating particular racial characteristics). The camera probes in on the leg and then cuts to the victim with a greedy curiosity: but the only response to what is supposed to be unbearable pain is that of a ham actor going through the motions of twisting his face.

One final example: at the top of a cliff the saboteurs have climbed (Gregory Peck crawls agonizingly towards us across a studio floor) is a solitary German guard. He is dressed in a huge, green-grey coat – the sequence is filmed in a mixture of blues and greens and greys. The assailants throw pebbles and make noises to frighten him and he becomes a slightly comic figure as he runs this way and that. Suddenly, we see him in a close-up with hands closing around his mouth : then the camera cuts away to show us a body falling spectacularly over the cliff and hitting the water. In a film which debates the morality of war, killing is *shown* to be fun.

To discover the full crudity of a film like *The Guns of Navarone* it would be necessary to analyse in much greater detail the style of the film – the complete absence of feeling or subtlety in the acting, for example, the deliberate garishness and vulgarity of the colours, the harsh and melodramatic lighting, and the way, for instance, the gun-tunnel is filmed to look like something out of bad science fiction. But it is clear, even from this brief discussion, that this 'pure entertainment' film communicates attitudes which can easily be summed up: war is brutal but fun, the way to win it is to be as uncivilized as your enemies, and the qualities to admire in a person are toughness and insensitivity.

Compared with *The Guns of Navarone*, a musical like *The Young Ones* seems, at first sight, to be scarcely worth discussing. The film tells the story of a group of young people who try to raise the money to keep their Youth Club open. To do this, they put on a show in an old theatre one Sunday night. The show, like the film, is built round the pop singer, Cliff Richard.

The story of a musical rarely matters: what is important, as dancers like Fred Astaire and Gene Kelly, and directors like Stanley Donen have shown, is the gaiety, wit, and inventiveness of the singing and the dancing. In *The Young Ones*, the inventiveness is limited, although one sequence, when the Edwardian theatre is brought back to life in song and dance, has a certain amount of vitality and is an advance on almost anything before it in the British musical.

What makes the film worth examining, though, is its treatment of the 'teenager'. A few years ago, the director, Sidney J. Furie, made a film about the elopement of two young Canadians, in which he treated their relationship with some understanding. But in this film, he shows no interest in what young people are like. Instead, he takes the simplest image offered by the magazines and the pop music industry.

Take his treatment of love: a film about young people in whom, according to the theme song, 'the flame is strong' might well be expected to show some interest in the subject. But the only moment in the film when there is any hint that sexual feeling exists comes when the 'bad girl', a star imported to give the show publicity, forces Cliff Richard, during a rehearsal of a song, to caress her while his real girl friend looks on. The emotional implication is that sex is something nasty. Love, on the other hand, is linked with a completely different set of images – Cliff Richard sings the theme song during a visit to a beach in a fast sports car, and as a background to the song we see blue sea, blue sky, and water-ski-ing. We are in the world of a Butlin's holiday camp advertisement, or of 'People Love Players', where love is just something that goes along with other consumer goods.

Most important of all are the assumptions the film makes about what *matters* to young people. What matters is Cliff Richard and whether or not he will sing on the Sunday night show. The tension is built up through a number of sequences in which his voice is heard over a pirate radio. And when he finally appears, Furie places the camera directly in front of him as he stands on the stage and at a very low angle, shooting along the line of his legs and body up to his face. The effect of this is to turn Richard into a heroic, dominating figure – a towering but untouchable sex-symbol.

The image of Cliff Richard in this film is, in fact, exactly the image of the pop singer the magazines and record companies sell. The pop singer is always 'one of us'. He is ordinary working-class, without fancy ideas – only he has been lucky and now has the biggest car and the best collection of Italian suits. In the film, Cliff Richard, too, is 'one of us'. He fights to keep the club open: only he is also the son of the rich speculator who is trying to close it down. So we move in a world that is pictured as 'ordinary', but which has all the glamour of big business deals, long-distance telephone calls, sudden flights to Scotland, and luxury cars. And in the end, the rich speculator also turns out to be 'one of us', when father joins son in a shuffle on the stage. Once again, a 'pure entertainment' film communicates attitudes based on a whole set of social values.

The third film, *The Angry Silence*, is apparently quite different. One of the 'values of our civilization' is, presumably, moral courage, and *The Angry Silence* has as its hero an ordinary little man who refuses to come out on strike because he thinks the strike is wrong. He is an individual conscience standing out against the mob, and he is first sent to Coventry and then beaten up, so that he loses an eye. The film is obviously trying to make an attack on herd-like conformity.

If, however, we examine what the film communicates through its style, we become aware of a completely different level of feeling.

The tone is set by the film's opening sequence. A train steams into the station of an industrial town. A carriage door opens, and out steps a man, ferrety-featured, with horn-rimmed spectacles and a grim earnestness on his sad, 'intellectual' face. He walks out of the station and is picked up by a car, which turns out to be driven by a shop steward. There is an air of mystery. Over a meal, the stranger says nobody must know they've met before the following morning.

This stranger gets a job with surprising ease, and throughout the film, he stands there in the background, pulling the strings, using the self-important shop-steward as a mouthpiece, receiving orders by telephone from London, talking in sinister tones about rigging meetings ('He must be taught a lesson. No, but a real lesson'), manipulating strikes which have no visible cause. When the strike collapses, he sneaks back to the train, off, presumably, to cause more trouble elsewhere.

Who is this man at the heart of the film? Where has he come from? What are his motives (even Communists, if that's what he is, must have some)? How does he come to have such influence over the shop-steward? The questions are never even put, let alone answered. The truth is that the makers of the film aren't interested in the *real* origins of a wild-cat strike: they have accepted a conventional notion and embodied it in a stock figure.

In the same way, they have accepted the sensational

newspaper picture of a strike, all lawlessness and violence and expressed it in a series of isolated, melodramatic shots. The central emotion is fear of the mob, and as the camera cuts dramatically from a stone through a window to a smashed-up bicycle and a burning car, all hackneyed images of violence, the deeper rhythms of a strike – the boredom, men with not much money to spend hanging around pubs, families worried about the latest instalment on the telly – are never investigated.

As a result of this basic lack of concern, there is a feeling of emptiness and unreality hanging over the film. There is, for example, a scene in the factory canteen, after Curtis, the blackleg, has been sent to Coventry. Curtis sits alone at a table. He looks round the room at other people talking and laughing – the camera pans round the tables following his gaze. Gradually, he begins to feel that they are laughing at him: the camera moves round faster, then tilts, in a drunken lurch, with nightmare close-ups of laughing, maniac faces, until Curtis jumps to his feet, bangs the table and yells, 'Shut up!' A strange stillness descends on the room – the verbal cliché I have just used expresses precisely the visual cliché of the film, and everybody remains absolutely still while Curtis screams, 'I don't want you to talk to me!' And then the eyes follow him as he staggers out. There is a blown-up feeling – not a movement anywhere, not a spoon tinkling or the sound of a tea-cup. Everything is frozen in a hack, over-dramatic statement.

Again, when Curtis marches to work alone during the second strike, he walks along streets that are completely empty. The background of houses is authentic – you can see those black rows right across industrial England – but the streets are unnaturally deserted. His footsteps echo hollowly on the pavement as he goes towards the factory gate where a crowd watches his approach.

The film's attitude is most clearly revealed in the climax. Curtis is in hospital. Union leaders are trying to quell a riotous mob, but they fail until Curtis' only friend, Joe who has so far sat on the fence, redeems himself by beating the leading thug to pulp and dragging him in front of the crowd, which becomes – again the literary cliché – strangely calm.

Joe captures the thug – a teddy boy – by pursuing him on a motor-bike. Our indignation is first turned against the teddy boy in a short sequence showing Curtis in bed, his eye bandaged; and then we see Joe, in righteous fury on his motorbike, bearing down on a running man. We are, in fact, being called on to approve a violent power image. And it is in this that *The Angry Silence* gives itself away.

For the film purports to be an attack on conformity. *But it is entirely conformist itself*. It accepts the conformist image of Communists, shop-stewards, wildcat strikes, and sheep-like workers, and ends by gloating over the violence it sets out to condemn.

Above all, *The Angry Silence* sees people in terms of a mob to be manipulated – and in this it is a direct reflection of the way the makers of the film see their audience. For although the film ostensibly condemns those who manipulate, it is, in itself, a thorough-going exercise in manipulation. There is no attempt to work honestly at communicating the truth of human experience. One eye is always on the shock effect to be produced on the back stalls. The attitude is summed up completely in one calculated shot: we are shown a close-up of a drawing-pin being stuck into the eye of a child, and then the camera pulls back to reveal that what we are looking at is a newspaper cutting being placed on a notice-board.

The shot is a gratuitous attempt to manipulate our attention. It assumes that we can be kept interested only if we are yelled at. It is the work, not of an artist concerned with the truth of his communication, but of a salesman who feels he has to put something across. And this brings us back to the position of the film as an art that is dependent on industrial processes.

4

For what is striking, when we think again of the three films I have described, is not the differences between them, but the ways in which they are alike. One is a war film, one a musical, and one a film of social comment. Yet they share certain qualities of tone and feeling.

111

Firstly, although all these films are, as I have shown, involved with the 'values of our civilization', they all of them offer an extreme simplification of experience. The strike, for example, in *The Angry Silence*, is so clearly ridiculous that the moral complexities surrounding the issue of private conscience and loyalty to the group can never be approached; while in *The Guns of Navarone* war, in spite of the apparent ironies, is no more than a boy-scout adventure. Instead of being invited to explore experience, we are asked in these films to respond to a set of empty conventions: heroism is gritting your teeth, jutting out your jaw and looking solemn; death is anonymous creatures in green uniforms being mown down by the score.

Secondly, the simplified versions of experience presented in these films reflect prejudices and assumptions that are shared by large numbers of people. These prejudices are taken and thrown back at us in a particularly crude form. So, if there is to be a strike, it will be violent, because that is the way we usually think of strikes; and the violence will be committed by a teddy boy, because that is the way we think of teddy boys. And if there is a Nazi, he will be a blond, blue-eyed sadist. (Compare the Nazi leaders in a documentary like *Mein Kampf*. They are all the more terrifying for being so obviously human.) There is, as a result, a constant pressure towards the hardening of assumptions that are already generally held.

Thirdly, on examination, these simplified versions turn out to be offered, not only by these three films, but by many of the other forms of mass communication. The importance of a pop singer is not exaggerated in a single, isolated film; the film reinforces an idea that is already there, on the radio, in the record industry, in the gossip columns and the magazines. The image of the unofficial strike in *The Angry Silence* is lifted straight out of the headlines of the tabloid Press. Turn from *The Guns of Navarone* to a *News of the World* story about a Japanese prison camp where there is a 'hate-crazed Jap fanatic' with 'a face like a jaundiced baboon', and you find this account of the torture of a girl: 'This tormentor ripped the girl's coat until she was half-naked, and the exposure caused the girl's

eyes to fill with tears.' A fantasy world is being given reality
by the repeated insistence with which it is presented.

This tendency to reduce experience to a formula which fits
our most commonplace assumptions can only contribute in
the end to the fixing of sharply defined limits of taste and
awareness. Anything which questions the commonplace or
challenges the imagination is likely to be discouraged.

It is this processing of experience that we need to be aware
of in confronting the typical products of the film industry.
The accusations that have been made against the cinema –
that it causes juvenile delinquency and sexual misbehaviour –
are not supported by any reliable evidence. But it is much more
difficult to measure the effects of the constant presentation of a
simplified and mechanical pattern of behaviour, and of a
repeated set of crude assumptions and attitudes. There is no
question of measuring off a single film against 'real life'; the
attitudes belong to a wider picture presented by the media in
general; and this general picture becomes itself an important
part of the reality that helps to shape our lives.

The point is, perhaps, most clearly made in a short film
called *Nice Time*, a documentary which gives a very personal
picture of Piccadilly at night. In this film we are shown two
young people holding hands in a cinema queue. They are
obviously in love – but behind them is a huge poster of Anita
Ekberg. And on the sound-track we hear love clichés from
the film they are going to see.

The implication is that a complex and living relationship
is being threatened and dominated by a crude stereotype. The
film the young people are waiting to see is offering them a
picture of love which is mechanical and belongs to a uniform
pattern, and this picture is imposed on their own experience.
The pressure is all the time towards a way of behaviour that
is conventional and lacking in spontaneity.

The image itself is, of course, over-simplified. It isolates the
cinema from all the other areas of experience that contribute
to the young people's knowledge of love. But in doing so it
makes us aware of one of the ways in which that knowledge
can be limited. And above all it calls attention to the inade-

quacy of the conventional film's response to human experience.

It is on the inadequacy of this response that the films I have described must ultimately be judged. A medium that has shown itself to be capable of extending awareness is being used to reflect the most obvious assumptions shared by the greatest number of people, assumptions which tend, in their turn, to be fixed by their own constant reflexion.

The passage I have quoted from *Nineteen Eighty-Four* – a passage which is, in some ways, frighteningly close to films like *The Guns of Navarone* – demonstrates the importance of the cinema in a society in which the rulers try to control the whole of experience. In Orwell's novel, the simplified picture of reality becomes real because of the totality with which it is created.

In our society, there are areas of experience outside. But it is important to be aware of the pressures towards stereotyped and conventional ways of thinking and feeling which are there in the typical 'pure entertainment' films we have been examining.

5

I have discussed these films in some detail because they seem to me to be representative of a general attitude in the industry. In each case, the form of the film communication has been dictated by economic pressures. As film costs rise, it becomes increasingly necessary to aim for the widest possible audience. And since only the familiar is safe, any experiment which involves risk becomes more and more difficult. Even the more enterprising British films in recent years, such as *Room at the Top*, *Saturday Night and Sunday Morning*, and *A Taste of Honey*, have been adaptations from best-sellers or stage successes. And although, compared with the films we have been analysing, these productions are fresh and honest in the way they look at contemporary life, they are all, to some extent, limited by the climate in which they have been made. *Room at the Top*, for example, falls back in the closing sequences on cliché violence and self-pity. Joe Lampton, the hero, gets drunk

THE FILM

after the woman he has rejected is killed in a car crash, and
is beaten up. (In the novel, he deals with his assailants with
commando skill.) He comes round to see a child pushing a
toy car over the edge of a heap of dirt. The audience, which
should be judging Joe, is given an easy bit of sentimentality.
In the same way, the relationships which Shelagh Delaney
has established with such clear-cut precision in her play are
almost bogged down in the literalness of Tony Richardson's
film, because we have to be given a number of 'cinematic' set
pieces – picturesque shots of boats on the Manchester ship
canal, a trip around Blackpool, a visit to the Derbyshire caves.
Even *Saturday Night and Sunday Morning,* in most ways an
honest and truthful though pedestrian film, scales down
Arthur Seaton's violent rebellion against the society around
him by giving undue emphasis to a comic feud with a gossipy
neighbour whose vast behind he peppers with a shot-gun. The
episode is in the traditional conventions of British comedy.
(There are signs elsewhere that Karel Reisz, the director, is
afraid of the *reality* of violence that makes the driving force
of Sillitoe's novel. The actual beating up of Arthur, by the
outraged husband's friends, is filmed so conventionally as to be
meaningless; and in his other film, *We Are the Lambeth Boys*,
about a Youth Club in Lambeth, Reisz carefully avoids any suggestion that young people are growing up in a violent world.)

The area of experiment in even the best British films is, in
fact, very limited. It is something that working-class characters
are no longer figures of fun. But there has been nothing in our
commercial cinema as experimental as, say, the BBC's *Goon
Show*, which ran for two years to a minority audience before
becoming one of the most popular programmes on the air –
and which proved in doing so that minority taste isn't static.
Given the opportunity, minorities might grow; but the economic structure of the film industry makes it difficult for the
opportunity to be given.

And yet it would be dangerous to dismiss the commercial
cinema, as those concerned with education sometimes tend to
do. Even inside the system, worthwhile films still get made. To
label films in categories – westerns, musicals, war-films,

115

thrillers – and then write them all off is to cut oneself off from many of the good things that the cinema has to offer.

To come back to the question of violence, for example. Educationists tend to assume that people need to be protected from any experience of violence on the screen. Yet in a film like *Paths of Glory*, the theme of violent death becomes a moral statement. When Kubrick shows us a public execution, he makes us intensely aware of a moral obscenity. In sharp, clear-cut images, he shows us three men on their way to be shot – one of them unconscious on a stretcher, one, who has achieved some sort of control, walking almost blindly along, staring straight in front, and the third, a tall, gangling man, twisting his head from side to side and whimpering like a frightened animal as a priest trots ineffectually alongside reciting words of comfort. The camera picks up, as if in passing, the assembled lines of soldiers, a Press photographer, the face of their Colonel. On the sound-track, drums beat louder and louder as the men are tied up and offered blindfolds. Before the order to fire is given, the drums stop, and in the silence Kubrick places us behind the firing squad. As the bullets strike and the bodies twitch, there is a momentary twitter of birds – and then we are suddenly back with the generals having breakfast.

There is no suggestion in such a sequence of violence for kicks. The light is sharp and clear, there is an austere concentration on essentials, and the effect is one of cold anger. In complete contrast to what happens in *The Guns of Navarone*, death becomes immediate and painful.

Again, compare the raucous, conventional treatment of violent hatred in *The Angry Silence* with the sensitive response to a similar subject – racial hatred – in Buñuel's *The Young One* – a film which the distributors have, incidentally, re-named *Island of Shame* and sent round the circuits as part of a horror programme. The film was shot very quickly on a cheap budget. The acting is, for the most part, poor; the script is often naïve; and the story of a Negro jazz musician who, wrongly accused of raping a white woman, takes refuge on an island occupied only by a racialist game-warden and a young girl, could have been sensational. But in Buñuel's hands it becomes an exploration of how human beings grow in understanding.

The violence is not evaded, as in Reisz's films. It is there all the time below the surface, and it flares out in the conflict between the Negro and Miller, the game-warden. But it is linked with a lack of maturity. As Miller grows in awareness of himself and other people, his racialism begins to crack.

This awareness develops through his relationship with Ewie, the young girl whose father has just died at the beginning of the film. At first Miller sees her only as a desirable object. He can't enter into any feelings she may have about the death of her father: we see him brushing her hair, dressing her in attractive clothes, caressing her on his knee, but casually hitting her when she spoils some food. But after Miller has made love to her – seduced would be too strong a word for the gentle tone in which the sequence is filmed – he gradually becomes aware of her as a person for whom he feels tenderness. Buñuel shows the first break in Miller's racialism when another white man tries to strike Ewie for having helped the Negro to escape. Miller stops him.

And in his treatment of sex, as well as violence, Buñuel shows a sense of complexity. Instead of the cliché image of a deceived young girl, he presents a human being, balanced between innocence and experience. Ewie has the innocence of a child – she can't understand why the Negro should insist on her covering her shoulders after she has taken a shower; and when Miller first kisses her, her response is to rough up her hair which he has so carefully brushed into place. But she is also a maturing woman. One shot at the end of the film places her with precision. We see her walking across the jetty, about to leave the island. She is in her new clothes, but she is a little clumsy in her high heels. Suddenly, she stops walking, and the camera cuts in close to her feet to show her hopping in a swift zig-zag between the cracks. She is joyful at leaving her childhood behind; but the joy is expressed in the gesture of a child.

I have called attention to this film for two reasons. Firstly, it is an indication of what an imaginative director can do, even when he is forced to work with economic limitations. And, secondly, it emphasizes the fact that it is the *treatment* of a subject that we need to examine when we look at a film. By his ability to project, in cinematic language, the contradictions and complexities of relationships between people, Buñuel has dealt with sex and violence in a way that is far removed from the crudities of the newspaper headlines, and has used them to extend our own understanding.

A third point might be made: the distribution companies have tried to bring this particular film back inside the conventions by selling it as a film of – sex and violence. In the same way, they advertised *Rocco and his Brothers* with huge posters crying 'Murder! Rape!' The defence was that in this way they were persuading the public to see a masterpiece.

But if you go to see murder and rape, rape and murder are what you are likely to respond to; a fact which makes it all the more important to bring to the screen an active critical judgement.

6

How are we to develop such judgement? In the absence of any established critical standards, there is no easy answer. In dealing with the culture of the past, we are helped by the fact that only the reasonably worthwhile will have survived. But in the cinema, where we are surrounded by a mass of material, most of it worthless, we have only our experience to guide us. Even those whom one would expect to be most helpful – the film critics of the 'quality' Press – have often assumed a tone of intellectual superiority about the medium, preferring to write slick, amusing columns about bad films, rather than to explain the reasons for their badness.

Yet the first step towards using the film positively must be the creation of standards. By this, I don't mean taking what the distribution catalogues sometimes call 'Film Classics' – adaptations of Shakespeare and Dickens – and seeing how they measure up to the originals; or doing a history of the cinema, with an emphasis on those silent films which are old and remote enough to have acquired an aura of cultural respectability; or studying film technique – it is possible, as the Orwell quotation shows, to be aware of technical achievements without being able to make any judgement about the quality of the experience that is being offered.

The creation of standards involves the building up of a critical response based on an awareness of how film works. And this depends, to begin with, on a willingness to look at films in a much more careful and critical way. The circumstances of cinema-going discourage such attention: in an atmosphere where there are constant distractions, it is much easier to respond to the familiar, to allow oneself to be washed over by the huge, imposing images on the screen, than to remain intellectually alive and questioning. But the cultivation of such attention is important, and it leads at once to a much more active enjoyment of what the cinema has to offer.

There are several ways in which this attention can be focused. Through discussion, for example, it becomes possible to re-create and explore the experience of a film. Such discussion, to be useful, must be based on the concrete details of what has been seen: it is tempting to use a film like *Paths of Glory* as the excuse for a sermon about the futility of war; but this would not help to build up a critical response to the film. What matters is what has appeared on the screen. In *The Guns of Navarone*, for instance, how are we put on the side of the officer in command, as played by Gregory Peck? What are we invited to admire in him? Such questions lead inevitably to a consideration of the *cinematic* qualities, for we know this man only through what we see – through the actions, words, movements, gestures and facial expressions of the actor, and through the way he is photographed; and our feelings are also affected by the music on the sound-track. It is by exploring these details that we sharpen our critical judgement – a judgement that can be developed further if we set this film alongside others that deal with war in a more serious way.

This kind of attention involves a careful and detailed scrutiny of films. Unfortunately, such a scrutiny is often difficult. The film exists only as a series of fleeting images, and it is normally impossible to go back and examine what one has just seen. This makes it all the more important to bring the film out of the commercial cinema and into the classroom or the youth group or the community centre where a more detailed examination and a directed discussion become possible. But at the same time it is important not to create the idea that film is just one more academic subject: it is better to know what, in the way of good or bad, the local cinema is offering than to show *Henry V* once a year.

It is, in fact, absurd that an art form of such potentiality should still be neglected in liberal education. Nobody asks why we teach music and drama: and nobody should ask why we teach film. But the approach is vital. The aim must be the development of a living response to films of all kinds. This does not mean that the latest musical can be measured against *L'Atalante*. But it does mean that we must be prepared to look at the latest musical critically, searching for freshness and life, and rejecting the mechanical and the dead.

I have emphasized the positive exploration of the film as a means of extending imaginative experience. In any education aimed at developing people critical of the assumptions of their environment, such a study would no doubt be linked with teaching about the other mass media.

But as I said at the beginning, film is not just one more of the media. It is a new and important art, which has already produced works of real stature, the study of which would contribute to the growth of understanding. It is up to those of us who care about our culture to see that this medium is not narrowed down by those whose interests and values are not compatible with our own.

Note: For a more detailed analysis of Buñuel's film see Alan Lovell's *The Anarchist Cinema*, from which some of these comments have been drawn.

*

ADDRESSES

British Film Institute: 81, Dean Street, London, W1

Anyone interested in film education would be well advised

to contact the Institute – the Education Officer is Paddy Whannel. The Institute has a Lecture Service, a Film Distribution Library, a Reference Library, and publishes a quarterly journal, *Sight and Sound*. Particularly useful from a teaching point of view is the selection of study extracts and short films which can be hired.

Society for Education in Film and Television: 7, Cumberland Close, Twickenham, Middlesex.

Amongst other activities, SEFT publishes *Screen Education*, and gives advice about films to hire and film-making in schools.

SOME USEFUL SHORT FILMS

A Time out of War	G.B.
Thursday's Children	G.B. or B.F.I.
Nice Time	Curzon Film Distributors
Hotel des Invalides	B.F.I. (in French)
The Visit	Contemporary
Living Jazz	B.F.I.
We Are the Lambeth Boys	Ford Film Library
Lonely Boy	B.F.I.

BOOKS AND PAMPHLETS

There are plenty of books giving information about film history and film techniques, and the social influence of film, but there is very little detailed critical analysis. The following books contain useful information:

BELA BELAZS, *Theory of the Film* (Dennis Dobson). A general book on film aesthetics.

ARTHUR KNIGHT, *The Liveliest Art* (Macmillan, N. York). Informative but uncritical.

PAUL ROTHA & RICHARD GRIFFITH, *The Film Till Now* (Vision Press). A detailed film history.

Rotha on Film (Faber). Useful information on the film industry.

ROGER MANVELL, *The Film and the Public* and *Film* (Penguin). Useful basic information, but the books have dated, and the critical attitude lacks direction.

LILLIAN ROSS, *Picture* (Gollancz & Penguin). A gossipy, journalistic book, which, however, offers an account of the difficulties of making a serious film in Hollywood.

PENELOPE HOUSTON: *The Contemporary Cinema* (Penguin).

A number of works of fiction explore the Hollywood world:

SCOTT FITZGERALD, *The Last Tycoon* (Penguin).

GAVIN LAMBERT, *The Slide Area* (Hamish Hamilton). Both the above works present a serious picture of Hollywood life.

Three particularly helpful pamphlets, obtainable from the British Film Institute are:

ALAN LOVELL, *The Anarchist Cinema*. This critical analysis of the films of Vigo, Franju, and Buñuel is valuable not only for its comments on actual films, but as an example of the way in which film analysis needs to be approached.

Film and Television in Education for Teaching. A report intended for Colleges and Departments of Education, but full of useful general information.

Teaching Film. An account of recent experiments in film teaching.

6   Magazines

DAVID HOLBROOK

Every day in the local paper shop the assistants dispatch a
large pile of periodicals. Among them are technical papers,
such as the *Grocer's Gazette* and the *Illustrated Carpenter and
Builder*. There are papers for members of small sects and
groups: *Dziennik Polska, Trade News*, the *Methodist Recor-
der*. There are children's papers: *Tiger, Robin, Look and
Learn*. There are women's papers – most are women's papers:
Woman, Woman's Realm, Nursery World, The Lady. There
are men's papers: *Farmer's Weekly* and the *Motor Cycle*. And
there are girls' papers: *Christian Novels, Red Letter, Mirabelle*. Others such as *Weekend, Today, Reveille*, and *Titbits*
are taken for whole families. And among all these are a minority of papers – usually only strictly on order – which represent
a minority 'serious' interest – the *Listener*, the *New Statesman*,
the *Spectator* and so on. The *Writer's and Artist's Yearbook*
lists about 700 journals – and this omits both local papers and
such trade and technical papers as the *Fish Fryer's Gazette*
(though it does include the *Funeral Service Journal*).

Some of these magazines are remarkable achievements of
technical skill – as is *Vogue,* for instance. Printers, typog-
raphers, photographers, block-makers, art directors, and editors, all are highly skilled, and produce with accuracy and
regularity millions of copies of beautifully printed magazines.
Many, like *Marilyn* and *Mirabelle* are, by comparison, inferior
products – some twenty-eight pages of unevenly printed matter, with indistinct half-tone blocks, poor typography, crude
drawings on yellowish-grey newsprint, much of the copy put
together from handouts from the publicity offices of 'pop' star
promoters such as Larry Parnes. In between these extremes
come all sorts: respectable papers, mediocre in appearance if

efficiently produced, such as *Woman's Mirror*; colourful and untidy sensational papers, such as *Today*; and crudely produced papers, with poor impressions of saucy 'cheese-cake', and yellowish-grey copy, such as *Reveille*.

But even in many of the popular papers some of the articles impress one with the effort the contents must have taken (e.g. 'You're going to be a new woman – fitter, slimmer, healthier – because you've discovered that FITNESS IS FUN. Now continue your exercise programme under Dr Warren Guild's expert guidance ...' or 'Under Canvas ... holiday in a tent. By parents of a two-year-old boy', both from *Woman's Mirror*). Of course, this becomes true the more a periodical is a technical paper or a paper for specialists – obviously, to write an article for *Farmer's Weekly*, or the *Illustrated Carpenter and Builder*, a contributor must not only be able to write, but the writer must know his subject at first hand, or near enough first hand. Of this most useful, informative, and instructive kind of periodical press, Great Britain probably has the most varied and, numerically, the largest-selling in the world. Such publications are a most valuable element in an educated democracy, and some represent important sectional groups who study and protect their own interests keenly and vigilantly. It was a small group of local anglers who some years ago won their case against Derby Corporation over river pollution, and forced the installation of purifying plant costing a million pounds: such incidents, a mark of health in the community, are often the result of a sense of cohesion, and an understanding of issues, rights, and courses of action, among those interested in a particular field. These interests are expressed and championed by their specialist press. So, apart from an occasional objection to their tendency towards typographical conservatism and mediocrity, one has nothing but respect for such periodicals as the *Accountant*, *Aeromodeller*, *Aeronautics*, the *Amateur Cine World*, *Amateur Gardening*, the *Amateur Historian*, the *Amateur Stage*, *Angling*, *Animal Ways*, the *Antique Collector*, *Apollo*, the *Aquarist and Pond-keeper*, and so on throughout the alphabet, right down to the *Yachtsman*. To these we may add such recent journalistic manifestations of practical critical attitudes to our kind of society as *Which?*, *Where?* and such papers. Besides these there are also many sound journals produced for professional groups or small minorities, such as the *Architectural Review*, the *Musical Times*, *Geological Magazine*, and the *Lancet*. Many of these are valuable in that they represent a disinterested preoccupation with the best that is thought and known about their subject.

But these valuable professional and minority publications, mostly with a sectional readership, do not represent the major cultural influence of periodical publication in England today. They do not form a general arena for the exchange of opinion: nor on the other hand do they represent the general level of mass-sale magazines. Yet they are probably the most important section of all periodical journalism, nowadays, in terms of the most positive and effective irrigation of public interest and opinion.

Indeed, they seem now to be of more positive value, in translating opinion into action and change, than the papers commonly accepted as those which serve the function of political debate, polemic, criticism, and the irrigation of public opinion among an informed and effective minority. There is no space to substantiate this opinion, which will almost certainly be judged eccentric. But the reader may care to compare some of the leading critical journals of the nineteenth century such as the *Westminster Review* or the *Quarterly Review* – available in some central and most university libraries – with our weeklies. The assumptions are very different, and so are the standards. The nineteenth century middle-class minority was not negligible numerically (the total readership was estimated as 220,000 in 1812 in a population of about 10,000,000, 1,000,000 of whom lived in London). Its attitudes to public views, points of morale and attitudes to life, and to cultural matters were responsible and 'meant'. By contrast our periodicals seem much more concerned, even at minority level, with entertainment rather than the 'irrigation of public opinion'. Entertainment demands that the writers and reviewers, as George Eliot once complained, 'must always be saying bright things', and this is not always compatible with adherence to principles, and the disinterested view. Reviewing is particularly deficient in standards of disinterestedness, though some shortcomings may simply be attributed to shortage of space, time, and payment, and there are many distinguished exceptions.

But, increasingly, the journals of critical opinion are influenced by trends towards sensationalism and triviality in the mass media, with which they have to compete. As the reader will know, there is for instance a kind of article, at all levels, and a kind of television programme, which appears to raise 'grave' and 'deep' issues. But when one examines such a feature as *Daily Mirror* 'shock issues' one finds that the reason for exploring the theme has no sincere impulse – either to explore the nature of reality, to gain insight into human nature, to find the truth, or to seek to persuade others to help put it right. Things are 'exposed', to arouse feelings of anger, disgust, or disquiet – but not to direct these in socially effective or even compassionate directions. Feelings are really aroused *to sell the journals*, or 'hold' an audience. An example at a popular level will be examined later: but at the 'serious' level such articles are found more frequently, nowadays, too. (One may study this trend in the *Guardian* since it moved to London.)

As an instance of the kind of tendency as one meets it, the present writer once hastily withdrew from a 'prestige' television programme when it became obvious that the producers wanted to use the text and drawings of the work of a disturbed child for sensational purposes, but were unwilling to allow proper time for this example to be qualified by comment. This is a typical and recurrent situation for anyone who writes.

Meanwhile, by compromise and a certain suspension of conscience and integrity; by 'brightness', by *facherie* – a kind of deliberate rudeness and by the display of a carefully calculated 'persona', the journalist who is less troubled by doubt and disinterested opinion gains rapid influence, and the 'serious' weekly merges thus into the world of popular journalism. (There is no need to mention the names of those who move with equal lack of grace and true conviction from television, to the *Spectator*, *Punch*, or the *Daily Express*.)

Inevitably, in such a situation, it becomes more difficult for any group of writers to stand outside the trends of popular journalism, and the trends of society itself, to pass comment and judgement. The pyrotechnic derisiveness of such a paper as *Private Eye* marks a new stage in the abrogation of a 'point of view' altogether, and of the need for moral positives behind social satire or journalism. In this situation, while there are many responsible and sincere articles and reviews in them, it may be said that the world of English culture, thought, and opinion would lose too little if such papers as the *New Statesman*, *Listener*, *Spectator*, *The Times Literary Supplement*, and the 'posh' Sunday papers closed tomorrow. There is an urgent need for the intellectual pretensions of these papers to be questioned: they are by no means as in touch with 'the best that is known and thought in the world' as they would wish to make us believe. Nor is such a paper as *Encounter*.

At best the writing in the most serious papers is done by people who seek to pursue a subject or express an opinion because they believe in it rather than seek 'success' or notoriety, though it is difficult to say even this with confidence nowadays. 'Meant' material obviously finds it harder and harder to find a home. The reader may try to compile a list of journals which seem to him free from the above strictures. Mine would include the following: *Architectural Review*; *Athene*; *New Era*; *Musical Times*; *Contemporary Review*; *Economist*; *Design*; *Essays in Criticism*; *The Use of English*; *Geological Magazine*; the *Lancet*; *Mind*; the *New Scientist*; *Universities Quarterly*; *Political Quarterly*; *Which?*; *History Today*; and perhaps *New Society*.

There are others which are neither corrupt nor commercial but unreliable and varying. There are political papers which vary according to the colour of the editor in charge for the time being, such as *New Left Review*. There are very small literary magazines such as *Outposts*; *Poetry Review*; *Stand* and *Delta* (which have received Arts Council grants). But the standard of production and writing in these is uncertain and often amateur, their values confused and provincial. Strangely enough one of the best pieces of periodical journalism I know is a provincial achievement – the Arts Page of the Bristol

Newspaper, the *Western Daily Press*. (This has now, however, been abandoned, for 'economic reasons'.)

There are also university journals and minority journals with circulations of about 2,000–10,000, their contributors unpaid. These come outside the scope of this essay, but their long-term influence – sometimes world-wide – should not be forgotten in the general picture. This is true of the best literary magazines of this kind in our century, the only equivalents in our time of the great nineteenth century papers, such as the *Calendar of Modern Letters* (1926-8), the *Criterion*, (which actually contains little one would want now to turn back to), the *Adelphi*, and particularly *Scrutiny* (1932–53) which has been reissued complete by Cambridge University Press because of its lasting value.

This is as much as can be said about 'quality' periodical publication in England now. We may turn now to the largest field of all periodical publication, which has close links with advertising, and with the popular periodical Press. Here there are main distinctions to be made, between smart, 'homely', and 'pop', but all belong to the same species. Their function is that of making a commercial return to the proprietors as a branch of the entertainments industry, closely linked with advertising and other departments of commerce. The 'smart' papers, such as *Vogue*, *House and Garden*, *Town*, *Queen*, *Tatler*, and (at a near 'pop' level) *Honey* have obvious links with the high-class furnishing, travel, fashion, clothes, cosmetics, and entertainments businesses. The 'respectable' or 'homely' journals consist of the many women's papers – *Woman*, *Woman and Beauty*, *Woman and Home*, *Woman and Shopping*, *Woman's Companion*, *Woman's Day*, *Woman's Illustrated*, *Woman's Journal*, *Woman's Mirror*, *Woman's Outlook*, *Woman's Own*, *Woman's Realm*, *Woman's Story Magazine*, *Woman's Weekly*, *Housewife*, *Homes and Gardens*, *House Beautiful*, and so on. These also link with fashions and cosmetics (but at a lower level of quality – Max Factor rather than Guerlain, as it were). They also help to sell a wide range of household goods, furniture, articles of hygiene, confectionery, and foodstuffs. The 'pop' papers range from *Reveille* to *Today* (previously *John Bull*) and carry low-level advertising of the kind one finds in such huge sale papers as the *Radio Times*. These are a chequer-work medley of skin balms, body builders (or slimming aids), forms of aspirin, books of etiquette, home-shopping catalogue agencies, 'The Exam Secret', shampoos, secretarial courses, schools of salesmanship, baldness cures, clothes, holidays, cosmetics, jewellery, guitars, wigs, bust developers ('Kurvon tablets'), and erotic underwear (The Famous Bare-a-Frontery, the Bikini Jama, Daring Golden Bra and G string, 'sizzling' Flamenco Bra and Briefs – 'gently urges your bust upwards into a youthful posture and inward for deepest cleavage … dramatically and tantalizingly overlaid with delicate black lace …', with a free can-can garter). Here we find ourselves in the weary world of commercial supplies for the Gerty MacDowells, for the romantic dreams of the urban adolescent: the sad fact being that any actual adolescent will reveal in imaginative work in school aspirations which are fine and noble; while nothing could be more ignoble than the prototype for whom the lowest grade periodicals and their seedy ads. are designed by the Leopold Blooms of today. As the editor of *Woman's Mirror* said recently 'everything starts with sex' – or, as one might translate this, commercial success depends upon exploiting acquisitive impulses, in a way which implies a poor regard for human nature and a recklessness as to the psychic consequences.

The link between these mass-sale papers, advertising, and commerce is made plain by advertisements in the national 'quality' Press, such as the following (with a drawing of a woman relaxing with a magazine).

SHOPPING STARTS HERE FOR 7¼ MILLION WOMEN

Week after week, in the colourful pages of WOMAN'S OWN, this woman, and 7,329,000 like her, find a combination of editorial and advertisement content which adds up to one of the world's most successful and trusted women's weeklies. At this moment, while relaxing with her favourite magazine, she's choosing her new clothes for Spring. In the women's mass market, WOMAN'S OWN sells everything a woman needs – and carries more advertisement pages, year after year, than any other women's magazine.

If you would like more detailed information about WOMAN'S
OWN *to assist you in the planning of your next campaign in the
women's mass market, please contact The Advertising Director,*

WOMAN'S OWN

– WHERE SHOPPING STARTS

The reader who has read Whitehead's contribution will be
aware of many necessary questions to be asked about the incidental cultural effects of advertising. In this advertisement
the link is revealed between advertising and the wider cultural
influence of popular reading matter: most of our periodical
Press consists of a particular kind of 'combination of editorial
and advertisement content'.

The clue to the nature of this popular periodical reading is
given by – 'successful', and especially 'trusted'. The other term
on which to fix one's attention is the word 'relaxed'. These
three terms in fact impose, universally, very considerable restrictions on the nature of the popular periodical Press – and
their freedom ever to become organs which help form public
opinion, to extend insight or understanding, or even to contribute much to the well-being of society. At best they are a
harmless form of distraction.

Why should this matter? What else could popular culture
offer?

From our culture and entertainment we can at best derive
a sense of human sympathy, insight into human nature, understanding of ideas and other kinds of experience, values and
standards, and a sense of significance. These, for instance, people once had, at a popular level, from Dickens and Bunyan.
Our society nowadays seems increasingly starved of these less
tangible human needs, of sources of sound nourishment for
the imagination, and of adequate concepts to help guide our
living. A periodical press could help to nourish such needs:
at best it does. The public library service, and such technical
developments as make it possible for us to buy university paper-
backs and Penguin Books, do provide such sound nourishment for mind and sensibility (the latter compete, of course,

with the lurid pulp book). The periodical press we have, however, is too content to substitute mere distraction for the pursuit of these better cultural satisfactions. Sometimes they supply falsifications of the nature of things which seem the reverse of helpful in living, and it seems that often the community has to preserve the arts of living *in spite of* the influence of the worst mass sale periodicals.

Commercial sales, 'trust' in a 'successful' magazine, and advertising, all demand a certain kind of attitude to life in the popular journal. It is on the whole falsely optimistic, and exaggeratedly idealized – the seas were never so blue as they are in *Vogue,* the women so elegant, the foreign places so halcyon: if a dirty old tramp or a camel are there, it is only to provide contrast with the image of an ideal – a bejewelled princess posing elegantly and impossibly by the moonlit wall (with a caption telling you where to purchase the clothes she is wearing). So it is, down through the women's magazines, where every face bears a smile and titled people appear in our midst, down to the glamorous boys and tousle-headed love-lorn girls in the strip stories of *Mirabelle* and *Marty*.

In this the magazines are playing on a human weakness, which perhaps may be explained in some such psychological terms as the following. In order to grow through his long childhood to full adult consciousness the human being is very dependent psychically on his parents. Because these parents are imperfect, being human, in order to tolerate their imperfections the child tends to seek to avoid distressing pain and fear, by inventing an ideal image, which, as it were, he 'throws over' the real and imperfect parents. In the subsequent conflict between appearance and reality, between the real and the ideal, lie the roots of all our psychic weaknesses: but the roots of all art, too. It is the price of human consciousness. To avoid reality if we can, because it requires painful adjustment – and 'growing up' – is one of our chief failings. But the creative processes of art help us to come closer to the real by delight and satisfaction, by refining our ideals, our visions, until they approximate more closely to reality. Through the visions of a Lawrence, or a Dickens, or a Degas, or a Gershwin or Stravinsky we may come closer to a true understanding of the nature of human nature, of ourselves and the world, not by comfort, but in joy. Of course, the process may involve discomforting changes in our attitudes but by such changes only are deep satisfactions gained.

Central and significant in this process of explaining the nature of experience is the image of woman as the embodiment of the good and the beautiful – from Botticelli's Venus, to Shakespeare's Cordelia, Degas' ballet-girls, and Dickens' Little Dorrit. And also, of course, our self-respect, our concepts of what things are good and desirable, and of what successful living may be, are often associated with images of a good self, and a good ideal – often a vision of the kind of woman we would like to serve – a muse, a goddess, a wife.

In the popular mind these concepts are largely established nowadays, alas, not so much by art, ceremony, or religion but by such influences as the periodical Press (along with television, advertising and the cinema). They are created by powerful images, the most important of which is the image of woman, from the *Vogue* models, to the teenage idols (such as Hayley Mills and Helen Shapiro) in the 'pop' magazines. The increasing use of pictures of women's faces and bodies in periodicals since the beginning of this century fulfils a particular need of a mass, suburban population in megalopolis, and touches on its peculiar neuroses. There is no conspiracy in this development – it happens unconsciously. But as an index of the condition of people's lives it suggests profound unhappiness and emotional disorder, that the ideals in popular culture are so thin, the concepts so reduced – at worst, what the Press themselves call ironically, 'cheesecake' – Barmecide.

The human mind, having become accustomed to hallucinate ideals in the process of psychic formation in childhood, tends to continue in adult life to idealize, and to throw appearances over reality, disguising the truth. So it is possible for people to live, as we vulgarly say, 'in a complete dream'. Since life is not a dream, the dream life inevitably clashes with reality, and if resources are not adequate to the shock, there will be a breakdown.

What part do popular entertainments play in this complex?

Most of our commercial periodical Press is devoted (like most 'pop' entertainment) to supplying forms of escape into hallucination to hide the drabness and insignificance of the commercial-industrial environment. The typical life of the dweller in megalopolis, because of the vast disorganized sprawl of the modern conurbation, is to dwell far out in an undistinguished community, ugly, insignificant, and shapeless on the ground. Those who go into the centre to work – daughters, sons, and fathers – travel in by tube or bus to offices and factories. There they are largely engaged in repetitive and insignificant tasks. From this they obtain relief by office flirtations, pin-up and pop-singer cults, film and television talk, cosmetic and fashion preoccupations. On these pursuits the modern office or factory worker often spends a disproportionate amount of income. At home the mother, alone in her comfortable, efficient, and hygienic living-box, suffers from isolation, frustration, and boredom. As the suburban dweller ranges farther out from the city centre the tedium and strain of commuter travel, the lack of significant occupation, the lack of vigorous family or community life, and the deficiency of creative leisure – all combine in their adverse influence, and their effects are felt increasingly in all great populations of suburban sprawls from Tokio to Greater London. This typical twentieth-century life is deficient in the numinous, the beautiful, in warmth of community, in human sympathy, means of creative expression, and means to discover a sense of significance in life through art, science, and creative leisure. It is in such conditions that the periodical Press of the popular kind establishes 'trust', and 'relaxation'. The first *Daily Mail* speaks in an editorial of being designed for commuter travel, in 1890. Editor and advertiser inculcate both desires for a dream-world, and then suggest that the path to the dream-world is in the main through the *acquisition* of personal possessions. This is a lie, and it is this deceit implicit in popular commercial entertainment which makes it unsatisfactory in terms of popular culture, and so distinct from the true arts and live entertainment.

The inculcation centres a good deal round the image of woman in a romantic setting and in romantic relationships, as in many advertisements and magazine stories. To achieve the ideal state of being suggested by this happy image you must be 'successful', suggests the periodical. Of course, the attraction is largely sexual – the reader 'wants' the girl lying on a bed on the cover of *Reveille*, or to kiss the happy inviting face on the cover of *Woman*. But the image is more than sexual – like the many images of women in classical paintings, or the many depictions in art of the Virgin Mary, it is a symbol of an ideal. But by contrast with the images of art, which express various degrees of altruism, aspiration, and devotion, the woman-image in popular journalism conveys *acquisitive* desirability, the impulse towards happy enjoyment essentially in terms of *possession*. The magazines convey 'the wants', and acquisitive attitudes to experience. The sexual impulse becomes for women readers a desire to 'be like that' – happy and desirable. In men readers it becomes a desire to possess that kind of relationship, and live that kind of bright, successful life. 'Success' lies in acquisition: the theme, of course, suits advertising and a mass production economy exactly. But it is a distortion. Both Bunyan and Dickens told their popular audiences that the greatest happiness comes from giving up preoccupations with material things altogether, and there is nothing acquisitive in folksong. Indeed, learning to love is in learning to *give*. In suggesting the reverse ('everything starts with sex') and by linking this with acquisitiveness much 'pop' culture is inimical to that self-fulfilment in personal relationships which every human being seeks.

Of course, when one's own circumstances are unhappy, tedious, insecure, and unattractive the magazine image of 'success' may deepen unhappiness and discontent. If people are influenced at all by the huge commercial entertainments industry they are surely likely to be worse at developing and cherishing real personal relationships? If they have any effect on living, the periodicals are likely to exacerbate those idealizing impulses by which we tend to become dissatisfied with our partners, with our real life, and with the exigencies of love, marriage, and parenthood, in favour of some hallucination – which exists

nowhere except between magazine covers or in our worst day-
dreams.

Moreover, the 'wants' inculcated by the periodicals, as we
know from personal observation of ourselves and others, do
tend to condition the behaviour of their readers in the direction of acquisitiveness, even in attempts to conquer the personal difficulties and conflicts between the ideal and the real. If
only the home is made gay, the wife given new clothes and
make-up, and we take a holiday in Italy ... Alas, the other
half of the equation – 'then we shall be happy' simply doesn't
follow, for reasons which would be obvious to a sociologist or
psychiatrist, but which are seldom pointed out in popular magazines. Of course, at the 'homely' level the advice and moral
implications of the contents of popular magazines are respectable, and largely sound. The women's mass-sale papers convey
a belief in the home and family, love and marriage, and traditional values to which one cannot object. They encourage
impulses towards self-respect, and mutual kindness and can
even suggest resistance to the misleading dream: here is the
typical 'reconciliation' end of a story in *Woman's Mirror*:
'*Keep a Dream Safe*', by Val Weeden:

He sat down beside her and put his arm around her shoulders.

"A dream," he said, "everybody needs a dream. When you get
ratty – no, don't deny it – I think of Louise. When I'm depressed, I
think of Louise. When I'm bored, I think of Louise. Twenty," he
said. "Young. Beautiful. Let her stay that way."

Nancy was silent. She wasn't sure that she liked the idea.

"That fellow," Bill said at last. "Mr Whatsit."

"Who?"

"Old pieface. That chap you were nearly engaged to."

"Frank," Nancy said. "Oh, him. What about him?"

"How do you think he feels about you?"

She didn't know. It had never occurred to her that Frank would
pay her a second thought.

"You know how you look?" he said. "Young. No lines here,"
he touched her forehead. "Happy. Smiling. That's the way you look
to him. For ever."

"Oh," Nancy said. It was an oddly comforting thought, almost as
if a sort of immortality had been bestowed on her.

"And you," he continued, "you have someone too. Everyone has."

And she knew that she did, and that it had all happened a long time ago, and that the young man's face was very dim now, but all the same he was a good escape hatch in time of need. The might-have-been that one never wanted.

"Yes," she admitted, "it's true."

"So – no Louise." Bill tapped his forehead. "I'll keep her up here." Then he leaned forward, touched the old green dress and said breezily: "But don't we look beautiful tonight! You and me both," and he ran his hand over his head. "All scented and shorn and beautiful. It seems a pity to waste us, we should be showing ourselves off."

He took her arm.

"Let's go out," he said, "and paint the town red."

But the implications about personal relationships are shallow.

The staple fare of the 'homely' popular journal is reassuring platitudes – at their most typical in Godfrey Winn (from the same issue):

What I mustn't forget to tell you before I sign off for another week, is about the carved wooden slogans hanging from the ceiling of The Pig and Whistle at Minehead, where everyone congregates in the evening, between dances.

I picked out three. One for husbands, one for wives, one for everyone. Here we go.

Try praising your wife ... even if it does frighten her at first.

A clever wife is the one who convinces her husband he is cleverer than she is.

If your face wants to smile, let it. If it doesn't, make it.

But you don't have to make it at Butlin's. At least I never have.

But, of course, the essence of such respectable moral attitudes is that the reader's 'relaxation' must not be disturbed. So there are many areas of opinion, insight, criticism, exploration of personal relationships, and *reality*, from which such 'homely' mass sale papers are excluded by their commercial exigencies, as are the Light Programme, and most television peak hour viewing. Thus, for example, the Problem Pages touch only slightly on common peccadilloes, rather more for their 'human interest' than for the advice itself. Their real intention is to hold the audience and sell the paper. A sub-editor who becomes too involved in the reality of some of the heart-rending problems sent in may be told (as a journalist I know was told) to 'forget it and make some up'. The main object of a periodical is to establish an ersatz trust, and to distract, rather than to act as a real clearing house for human troubles or even to offer positive help in living, such as a novelist who is an artist offers. (*Woman* receives 30,000 letters a month.)

Yet, of course, the apparent offer of 'help' and advice is a main plank in the popular periodical's appeal, and when it misuses this trust it seems to me most vicious. When the values are respectable, as in the mass 'homely' women's papers, one can only deplore the reduction of traditional values to the levels of platitudes which may be more enlightened than the old codes, but are often too superficial in their implicit attitudes to life. Even there, there are many misleading suggestions towards behaviour which might at best be ridiculous, at worst disastrous.

Flirting's fun! And it's high time the art came back. Men – and women – cannot live by bread alone! Let us practise the brief but charming art of lowering long lashes at an unexpected compliment ... the fleeting touch of the hand ... the quick turn of the head and flick of the lashes that leads a man to believe you and he share the same brilliant sense of humour. Yes, it's high time.

(101 ways to make yourself more exciting to look at, listen to, live with ... *Woman's Own*)

But elsewhere there are more questionable impulses at work, to establish 'trends', and the trends inculcated in the present-day younger generation seem to me socially very unfortunate. In this I find my disquiet reinforced by teaching experience over the last ten years: in recent years the child of twelve to fifteen has been approached on a large scale by commercial undertakings, investing large sums to secure their custom (at the rate, I believe, of something like six hundred million pounds a year). In this context it is as 'good business'

137

worth investing £10,000 in a new dance like the Twist, or in promoting a pop star, or in a fashion development such as frilly petticoats or wigs. Such a commercial promotion has been found, however, to work more successfully when it contains 'built in' to its appeal, a calculated antipathy to traditional authorities – parents and teachers – ('who are they to say?') and to traditional restraints on behaviour, as part of the inculcation of herd feeling. (Such underhand methods of promotion are probably imitated from America where the employment of psychology in commerce is more cynical. But even over here a 'pop' song writer will reveal – as an article in the *Guardian* cheerfully quoted – that 'the secret of success is to get the boy and girl into bed together without really saying so.')

Of course, 'trends' are a pattern of all mass advertising and commercial enterprises and the basis of them lies in the large expense of planning and promoting an industrial commercial enterprise in a mass production economy. But the creation of trends has become a cultural feature, at all levels, and is one which inhibits personal growth by seeking to submerge individuality in mass group stereotypes. People are encouraged to feel afraid of breaking the herd patterns, and thus becoming ostracized or isolated. They become less confident in their own good sense. In a mass suburban society, deficient in warmth of community, this inevitably exacerbates loneliness and the associated psychic disturbances. These trends are evident among young people nowadays as compared with those one taught in school ten years ago. Today they shrink from personal contact under the deafening noise of their music, at dances and youth clubs, whereas ten years ago it was easier to have a much more uninhibited social evening. One notices among young people nowadays, too, more compulsive relationships – one steady boyfriend who dominates the girl possessively – and in others one finds equally anxious early promiscuity. Young men are 'cool' to girls, discourteously so by the standards of 1940–50. There are many reasons for these changes, but in the degree to which they follow stereotype patterns (e.g. imitating Elvis's image-manner) they have been incidentally exacerbated by the promotion of herd cults and trends, by the assault on relationships with adults of an older generation, and in such things as the damage done to family life by television. 'Everybody does it' has become a powerful threat to traditional sanctions on personal behaviour.

A philosophical vindication of this promotion of 'freer' sexual trends has established itself in terms of a common belief that our psychic troubles are caused by 'restraints' imposed on our 'instincts' by 'society'. While this belief is of obvious value to an acquisitive commercial ethos, it belongs to Freudian psycho-biology of about 1908, and represents a view long ago discarded in psycho-analytical theory. Allport (1949), Cohen (1946), and Harry Guntrip are among psycho-analytical writers who have stated that we can no longer speak of 'instincts' in human behaviour, as man is too complex. The impulses (as in sex) which *some* find difficulty in controlling are rather 'neurotic drives', and failures of maturational processes. Society is an expression of man's best potentialities rather than a mere source of 'repression', and the origins of neuroses are now considered to be in the frustration of love in early infancy, rather than in any innate drives, or the restrictive effect of society. Many 'enlightened' trends, such as that towards toleration of pornography, and others supposed to belong to a 'new morality' do not in fact have their origins in any creditable source, but only in 'bright' journalistic notions. Intellectually such 'trends' are disastrous, because they inculcate a herd cohesion – 'being with it' – which inhibits fresh thought: they tend to fortify a collective defence against the discomforts of a closer approach to reality in new ideas. For instance, in the atmosphere of the prevalent adherence to Freudian pychobiology and the 'instinct' theory, it would be very difficult to promote the more optimistic attitude to maturational processes and human personality as put forward by more recent psycho-analytical writers such as D. W. Winnicott, D. W. R. Fairbairn, and Harry Guntrip, particularly as their views challenge the assumption that to 'free' 'instinct' is good.

The 'trend', as I have said, is a feature of literary taste, too. At lower levels the latest literary reputation is changed frequently: Sybille Bedford has lately replaced Laurence Durrell:

Vogue's regular cultural gesture called 'Faces and Places' (or something like that) is typical, though it probably seldom sells as much as one copy of any book mentioned. But even the *New Statesman* readership tends to need to 'wear' the latest literary opinion.*

At lower levels the inculcation of trends sells dances, records, kinds of shirt (stripey), kinds of coat (shiny black Bardot), holidays abroad (packaged winter sports, film-famous Greek islands), and people will often follow these trends, even when they cannot afford them, because they become afraid of exclusion, or failure, if they are not 'with it'. The underlying fear of being not 'with it' could possibly be linked with the fear of not manifesting the bright successful experience, such as is delineated in the images of those shapely girls, unruffled and never complaining, by those never-so-blue seas. The trend seekers may at the time, sadly enough, think they are 'setting' trends – whereas in fact, of course, they are sheepishly following advertiser's ploys, and a mass fashion.

The inculcation of trends in behaviour and the deliberate breaching of traditional and personal sanctions in behaviour begin in reading matter designed for children. The most alarming trend is towards sexual precocity. Here is an example from a girls' picture paper:

A KISS TO REMEMBER

★ It takes two to make a memorable kiss. You and him! So don't leave it all up to him. You need a little technique, too.

★ Don't stare at him. You'll only put him right off. Close your eyes and part your lips oh-so-slightly.

★ Kiss as though you really mean it . . .

★ Use the indelible kind. (Of lipstick.)

★ Soft . . . that's how your lips should feel under his . . .

★ . . . well, make it a kiss he'll remember. He'll come back for more.

There is no need to labour a verbal analysis. It is enough to say nothing is sacred to Fleet Street – not even the most

* A woman said to me at a party, 'Yes, I've read Wain's new book but I don't know what I think of it as it hasn't been reviewed yet.'

spontaneous, tender, and naïve of life's experiences, the first discovery of kissing. Here is the source of the precocious 'knowingness' of the adolescent that, as teachers know, does lead to personal disaster. But the writers don't care, any more than they care for the characters in the short stories they write, or for the incidental effects of their romantic compositions, and their implicit morality.

There are resistances in children, but where there is any weakness the natural safeguards perish in the pursuit of the trend stereotype that 'everybody does'. But the children are still children. Cynical journalism tends to interest them unduly in sexual experiences, only appropriate to adults who are ready for the complex consequences and responsibilities of such adventures. One knows at school how much, inwardly, the readers of such papers as *Marty*, *Mirabelle*, and *Roxy* are still children. But it is such influences which have so changed their behaviour, since the war, to the extent that a film show in school or youth club, for instance, is the occasion for public necking, in which the most disturbing element is its deliberate exhibitionism, as if the most important thing about love-making were that others should be made aware of it. This sexual precocity is now being promoted among children of 8–12. *Princess*, a paper for these ages, has inset features on 'pop' stars and their private lives, though, of course, its other copy is appropriately and properly childish.

Consider, as a further example, a paper like *Mirabelle*. Apart from a number of romantic strip cartoons and a few articles such papers contain a good deal of straight publicity material put out by the promoters of 'pop' singers. 'Trust' is established by Fan Club items, a horoscope ('love lucky dates are tomorrow (Tuesday) and Saturday'), and by features ostensibly offering advice from the 'pop' idols themselves – 'Ask Adam ... A Boy's View of A Girl's World' (*'When a boy whistles at me, can I whistle back?* No, he's supposed to be the wolf, remember. Try a slight smile to show you don't mind him 'whistling'.) On the centre pages Sylvia Ferguson asks Mark Wynter (star of *Just for Fun*) 'Are Engagements Square?' The

DISCRIMINATION AND POPULAR CULTURE

matter is mostly as respectable and fatuous as ever, except that
one can perceive in it the pressure of the huge 'pop'-singer promotion industry linked to the encouragement of 'teen-age'
anti-social attitudes, antipathy to 'them', and too early marriage.
In fact a high proportion of marriages under twenty are
breaking up, and the more subtle considerations of such a
subject are here deliberately ignored – not because the author
is unaware of them, but because the promotion of the 'music
industry' works better by encouraging sexual precocity, and
oversimple attitudes to sex. (By contrast, surely, *Marilyn*
would never disturb 'trust' and 'relaxation' by having an article
on the distressing increase of venereal diseases among today's
young people? Nor would it publish such remarkably excellent
comments on marriage as those of Dr Spock in the *Observer*?).

Like so many girls who dream of the moment they will become
engaged, Mark too has very romantic dreams of the time he will
ask a girl to become his wife.
   '*I think,*' he said, '*I'd like to propose over candle-lit dinner, in
the corner of a quiet restaurant, with an orchestra playing dreamy
music. That would be ideal – just great!*'
   Would he hold a big party to announce the engagement?
   'No, I wouldn't throw the occasion open to a party, because I
don't like parties. I think I'd feel rather proud if we were able to
keep it secret – just between ourselves.'

YOUNG MARRIAGES

   'And have you ever met a girl you would like to pop the question
to?' I asked.
   'No, I'm afraid I haven't – not yet,' he sighed. 'But I'd like to
get married while I'm still young. I'm not at all against young
marriages. I know of quite a few that have worked out very well.
   'I think teenagers are more sensible today than they were say
fifty years ago. They are given more responsibility and so they are
more independent. Years ago they were kept under the thumb. You
know, "children should be seen and not heard,"' he grinned.
   'Nowadays things are very different. Teenagers run the music
industry today, that's for a dead cert!'
   Mark went on, 'Marrying young means you grow up with your
children. I'd like that. I think young parents tend to have more
patience.'

Well, Mark is certainly one guy who likes the idea of engagements and the sentimental trimmings.

What do *you* think?

One of the more recent ploys of journalism directed at the young readers is to establish 'trust' by giving advice on sexual conduct. But in the context of excessive sex-consciousness, and because it is given for sensational reasons, the 'advice' is the reverse of helpful.

One magazine, addressed to intelligent twenty-year-olds, offers advice to the young – endless advice – about love and sex, as though there was nothing else in life but to be 'bright', and to possess the experience of sexual adventure. In real life, until sexual experience, desire takes its place in a large web of shared-togetherness, at all the civilized points of contact between man and woman, one hasn't *begun* to love. This paper, however, separates sexual awareness from this whole complex as a 'topic', in such a way that the sex-sophisticated and acquisitive copy merges unperceived into the ads: one cannot be a 'success' until one *has* certain experiences – and certain clothes and other possessions. Here are quotations: 'Are you ready for marriage?' 'How to be a hit at a dance', 'The art of small talk gets you more dates', 'Don't put on the big act or you'll fail', 'You too can sparkle by starlight', 'Do relax, you're here to enjoy yourself', 'It's fun to try a private moment', 'As every girl would agree, it's better to have boy-trouble than no-boy trouble'.

These are all from the text of one issue. The ad. copy cunningly takes the implications over to material acquisition. 'Only a seam can give the most elegant legs in the world', and so on. The purpose of the paper behind the helpful front, is to gain the 'trust' of a generation, to hold before them a pretend-world in which they will feel they cannot live successfully – and *love* successfully – without certain know-how – *and the equipment to go with it*.

The main plank of the confidence-gaining advice in magazines is on matters related to sexual conduct. The paper exudes sex advice, with the effect that it inflates in an obsessed way from the whole of life. Then the paper offers direct advice from an expert such as Dr Eustace Chesser. But this advice is utterly at odds with the general suggestion of the rest of the paper. The text and ads imply 'Sweep him off his feet' you are not with it unless you have wildly romantic experiences! But then a psychiatrist is roped in, for prestige and trust, to say 'wait'! But, of course, what he 'reveals', as of promiscuity, stimulates the mental consciousness, too. The culminating effect is to play on every chord of young people's psychic instability over sexual matters – for commercial ends, to gain 'trust'.

There was one very good piece in the first issue of one paper in the supplement, by Dr Keith Cameron:

I wouldn't for a moment suggest promiscuity or even the full expression of sex in any individual case, as part of the essential process of 'getting to know men'. Indeed, promiscuity will do just the opposite, because you can never have a total relationship that way at all. You simply isolate sex at the expense of everything else.

I'd go so far as to say that the promiscuous people are not on the whole over-sexed, but *under*-sexed; they have to keep trying to prove to themselves that they're 'normal'.

This is loose language for a psychological writer, but it seems to me closer to truth than anything else in the paper. In general a qualified frankness about sexual matters in periodicals may be valuable – though it is, of course, ridiculous to suppose that anyone's deeper potentialities in love can be improved by a few periodical articles! But, above all, Dr Cameron's remarks on immaturity *are true of this kind of paper itself*. They cannot help appearing to encourage 'promiscuous' appetite, suggesting all the time the presence and force of sex, to sell goods. Dr Cameron is merely employed to secure confidence by adding apparent respectability and paternal authority. He might well be horrified if he realized this. The journal's is the mountebank's trick, gaining trust to sell trash.

It is surely cruel, so to stimulate desire, acquisitiveness, and sex-consciousness – and then to produce the medical man to give a cold-blooded piece of advice on 'how to behave'. Too late! No medical man can have enough prestige, despite his 'frankness', to overcome the impression made by the rest of the magazine, with its whirl of bare thighs, straining bosoms, kissing mouths and romantic stories* – that the reader is a failure unless he or she is engaged in sexual adventure most of the time.

What kind of youth can it be, if one kisses according to *Marty*, and sees 'success' in terms merely of sexual adventure, according to *Mirabelle* and such?

It is interesting to consider who the people are who follow these formulae – probably unaware of the incidental harm they must inevitably do. What kind of person would be prepared to follow the definitions of 'the market's needs' as one finds in the *Writer's and Artist's Yearbook*:

... young, gay, lively ... we welcome fresh, original ideas from free-lance writers for Profiles, humour ... the art of living – *and loving*. If it's new, we are interested. Fiction: first-rate writing well plotted, with situations *and* problems *with which the reader can identify herself*. Particularly the short short story ...

(*My italics*)

'Happy endings' are essential, to preserve 'relaxation'. Identification is necessary to the promotion of a dream world, in which acquisitiveness and a desire to be 'with it' may be stimulated.

... Requires scripts for picture serials and complete picture stories *with emotional plots* and with the love interest maintained from first to last; *happy endings essential* ...

Imagine Tolstoy, D. H. Lawrence, Guy de Maupassant, Mark Twain, or Charles Dickens responding to the injunctions I have put in italics above, from Fleet Street!

While technical developments in magazine production have made great progress since the end of the last century, the content of this branch of popular entertainment has made few advances. It follows mostly the old-fashioned trivial paths. Indeed, on the whole, in most of the mass-sale popular periodicals, there has been a steady increase in triviality and distraction, forced on the papers by economic necessity. The same

* And a certain sophisticated suggestiveness that seems to verge on obscenity: e.g. cartoon of two girls going upstairs, caption 'I said to him I've got nothing to hide. ...'

145

is true, of course, of 'pop' fiction, programmes and serials over wireless and television, and the treatment of newspaper news. The stereotypes of the composition and presentation of such items of popular entertainment have hardly changed since the new journalism of the 1880s, and the invention of the new *Daily Mail*, *Tit-Bits*, and *Answers*. Of course there are some developments, such as the new bright, smart journal (such as *Town*, *Topic*, etc.), and the new 'frankness' about sex (often rather a near-pornography as in the pin-up papers), the new cult of irresponsible satire, without ideals or even a point of view. But fundamentally there is nothing more conservative than popular culture, and to read through a heap of magazines all announcing their up-to-date newness is to be wearily reminded of the old stock tricks of the journalist's trade. The proportion of good, serious, 'meant' and genuinely critical periodical journalism has meanwhile decreased.

To say so much is perhaps the first stage in resisting the self-attributed prestige of such a branch of the entertainment industry as the periodical Press. It does not develop in content and it is not really 'free': it is no more free than the proprietors' business requirements. One may compare the widespread developments in the content of education since 1900, with the surprising similarity between the papers such as *Weekend* or *Reveille* and their antecedents of the 1880s, and the Northcliffe revolution.

There has been some development of function. The old concept of a magazine as an area for the exchange of opinion and comment, and as a means to irrigate public opinion, died hard, with Northcliffe. Now most magazines, especially the mass-sale ones, are no more than entertainment, and nothing could be further from their function than discourse, argument, or the irrigation of opinion. Yet they do change attitudes – and they have contributed to the creation of a new kind of society – in terms largely of the purchasing of certain goods and equipment, and the pursuit of a certain material standard of living. With these they have inculcated certain attitudes to experience – certain codes of respectability, in social behaviour and in personal behaviour, many of which are unobjectionable, but many false. For, compared with what one knows of creative effort and energy in the community from working with children in school, these attitudes to experience, by contrast, lack depth. As a feature of popular culture, such journals contribute little to relieve the tedium and fundamental dissatisfactions of the featureless life of megalopolis and suburbia, lacking as it is in the thriving contacts of a live community. Yet one knows from how well children write themselves in English lessons in school how much potential – in terms of aspiration and ambition – lies unawakened in the community, and fails to be carried over from childhood to adulthood. Perhaps the worst thing about magazines is that they are so much below the level of really touching on people's real tastes and interests at all – they are taken and read as light distraction, and their effects are generally no more than that of promoting 'tumid apathy', indifference to public life, and to opinion and change. Culturally they promote only stereotypes at the 'lowest common denominator', in terms of concepts of what life can offer, and damaging hallucinations.

We may end by looking at a typical example, which sums up the essential triviality, the stimulation without satisfaction, the damage to language, the conservatism of the periodical Press at popular level. Such weary examples could be picked in dozens any day from a score of papers. This happens to be about the death of Von Trips, the motor-racing driver: 'True-life drama'. The news item was about a year old: but the skilful magazine writer drags the old story out for the sensational juice it can still yield, 'handled properly'. The method used is the typical one of popular journalism, from the *Daily Mirror* to the *News of the World*. The writer seeks to play upon the reader's fear of death – his natural preoccupation with the fact that 'in the midst of life we are in death'. It is the province of the poet: but the poet seeks to share his awareness with the readers, so that both may find purchase, a hold on experience, a way back to positive belief in the continuity of life, after grief at a bereavement, or in the face of mortality. Art is inevitably compassionate, because the creative writer is seeking by words to share his agony with others. All children – not

147

least 'backward' children – can be artist writers in this sense.

The popular magazine writer pretends to be using words for the same kind of end. He apparently implies that he is condemning the thing he writes about: he will title his feature THE HORROR OF PROSTITUTION; THE BITTER TRUTH ABOUT ADDICTION and so forth. But the excitement derives from what is *revealed*, rather than in what is engaged with. Here motor racing is called THIS CRUEL GAME but the excitement is derived from the excitements of motor-racing itself, particularly its liability to lead to maiming and death.

Though the writer *appears* to be telling his story in compassion for the protagonist and his family, and for those hurt and killed by the crash, he is in fact doing all he can to bring it back simply for public exhibition – to vicarious relish – by exploiting the most poignant and horrific moments of their suffering. He is not doing this for any serious purpose – to try to get motor racing banned, or made safer, or to defend it as a necessary blood-sport. He is certainly not concerned to help us to come to terms with the presence of death which is inevitable in our lives. He is simply playing on the reader's nerves – to hold him in distraction a little while, to fray his feelings – and then, having aroused him, leave him. This kind of attention suits both advertiser and the need of the paper to establish a habit.* The writer is arousing sadistic, morbid, and cruel feelings without helping the reader to gain order and control over them. Public executions and horror comics came to be prohibited because it came to be recognized that such stirrings of savage feelings had a degrading effect, to an extent which functioned against personal and public order and wellbeing. Yet the huge periodical industry nowadays deliberately and recklessly stirs sexual, sadistic, and morbid feeling with no care for the results. Commercial criteria are assumed to be the only ones involved.

Here are representative paragraphs designed to give such a juicy shock to the emotions as contrived by this kind of effic-

---

* Vance Packard I believe makes the point that television programmes which were 'too good' were found to alienate viewers to advertisements: advertising demands 'relaxation' in a context of mediocre entertainment.

ient journalism. The page is given to colour pictures, accidentally taken at the track, of Von Trips in his crashing car. The unfortunate driver can be seen in his seat, and one is invited to identify oneself with the man at the point of death ('As the crimson Ferrari rocketed on, Von Trips had a hundredth of a second to realize that this was the end'). Short of describing the actual maimings and terrible bodily wounds the writer squeezes the maximum horror from the incident. He builds up the lack of expectation in the spectators, with 'human interest':

Poppa Piero Carpani, grocer, and father of four, squinted anxiously at the sky before he made his big decision.

Neither Pierro, his wife nor the children, had ever seen a motor race before.

In the Ferrari pits at Monza, mechanics swarmed over the five blood-red cars, bearing the name of the famous Italian manufacturer.

And so was beautiful American millionairess Sally Ringling, twenty-seven-year-old daughter of one of the seven Ringling Circus brothers. Her friends called her 'race-crazy' – but this was one race Sally had not wanted to see.

Only a week before, she had flown back to America, filled with a ghastly presentiment of disaster. Then the cable arrived. It said: 'Come to Monza. I am going to win the World Championship. I want you to be there.' It was signed 'Wolfgang'.

Debonair Count Wolfgang Von Trips, ('Taffy' to his fellow drivers – 'Count Crash' to the crowds), had loved her from the moment they first met at the Le Mans twenty-four-hour race two years before.

On the morning of the big race, the pale, slim German nobleman proposed. And Sally accepted. But she was the unhappiest person of all the 50,000 who thronged the death-circuit on September 10, 1961.

Note that the race track is now the 'death circuit': both the writer and the reader know, in a cynical way, that all they are doing is treading their same old weary circuit of sensation-mongering with the subtle play on feelings about sex and death. The cars are 'locked in a crazy embrace', 'the Ferrari rocketed on'. Schoolboys can write pastiche of this kind of thing with great efficiency I find: one remembers the maxim attributed to Lord Northcliffe, 'our readers have a mental age of fourteen and a half'.

Then comes the meat. Of course, it 'holds one':

Von Trips had a hundredth of a second to realize that this was the end. He tried to free himself as the car spun through the air before spinning end over end on to the track.

The chances are that he never even *saw* the blur of horrified faces as his car slashed into the crowd. He was killed instantly when...

The 'Death Circuit' had claimed one of the greatest motor-racing drivers of all time. And fifteen men and women who went to see the fun.

There was no victor's laurel for Von Trips. But every three days for a month afterwards, a fresh red rose was found on the spot where he died – laid there by a young Milan student, Francesca Guadenzio.

'I was just a friend,' she said.

Such is the general level of diet in the popular journals in an educated democracy in 1964.

To anyone concerned with the health of the language, in relation to people's capacities to deal with life, what is distressing here is the banality, the commonplace quality of the cliché, and the crudity with which English words are handled here, from 'end', 'blood', and 'fun' to 'miracle', 'loved', and 'death'. This example is a typical one of hundreds poured out by Fleet Street every week. While this industry continues to be in hands indifferent to its inevitable moral influences it will continue to damage and weaken both language and attitudes to life at the popular level. Meanwhile at other levels things are not so much better that we can be proud of them.

The need to reform the minority Press and free it from the debasing influence of commercial pressures is urgent. But it seems unlikely that there is any hope of expecting any improvement, towards the level an educated public deserves, in a mass popular commercial periodical Press which has been content to follow the old Northcliffe formulae, profitably, for nearly a century: unless we accept that grave social consequences must inevitably come from the effect of leaving widespread and powerful cultural influences in the hands of those whose sole motives and responsibilities are commercial ones. To end this state of affairs is a large and necessary reform, and would require subtle legislation: yet only thus could the popular periodical Press become truly free enough to improve. Meanwhile it is left to the teacher in school to cooperate with young readers, to examine the fare 'pop' journalism offers them, to demonstrate to them that they can write all the varieties of 'features' much better themselves, and that there are other possibilities in life other than those so dismally and limitingly exhibited on the typical railway bookstall.

*

BOOKS

TOM CLARKE, *My Northcliffe Diary* (o.p.)

ANDOR GOMME, 'Criticism and the Reading Public' in *The Modern Age* (Pelican Guide to English Literature)

RICHARD HOGGART, *The Uses of Literacy* (Pelican)

D. HOLBROOK, *English for Maturity* (C.U.P.) for analysis of *Reveille*, and *The Secret Places* (Methuen) for analysis of teenage journals.

DEREK HUDSON, *British Journalists and Newspapers* (Collins) A short popular pictorial account.

Q. D. LEAVIS, *Fiction and the Reading Public* (o.p.)

GEORGE ORWELL, *Critical Essays* (Secker and Warburg)

J. B. WILLIAMS, *History of English Journalism*

DANIEL BOORSTIN, *The Image* (Pelican)

HARRY GUNTRIP, *Personality Structure and Human Interaction* (Hogarth). For a critique of Freudian psychobiology and the 'instinct theory'.

7   Recorded Music

DONALD HUGHES

1

It needs considerable imagination today to realize how difficult it was for anyone interested in music at the beginning of
the century to follow up that interest. If you lived anywhere
outside the very largest cities, you could have very little musical
experience beyond what you made yourself. Professional concerts were rarer even than they are today; there might be a
music-hall in the nearest centre of population, and in a cathe-
dral city you could hear choral music. In the North there
would be the town or factory brass band. Even if you played or
sang yourself, comparatively little music was available in cheap
printed editions much before the turn of the century.

This is why all children in respectable middle-class homes
in Victorian and early twentieth-century England were expected to learn the piano. How else could they get musical experience? Obviously they could not join in the music-hall and
public house songs. Later on they could join the local choral
or operatic society and sing 'Messiah' or 'The Mikado'. But
in general, music, except what you sang in the bath, was a
scarce commodity.

Now it is an axiom of economics that scarcity creates value.
A man in the middle of the Sahara may be prepared to give
a fortune for a glass of water that he would expect for nothing
in a London restaurant. And a music-lover of the nineteenth
century might have to make, and would probably be willing to
make, considerable sacrifices of time and money to follow his
hobby.

The arrival of the radio and record-player has made an almost unbelievable difference to this situation. For some people

it has become a question not so much of sacrificing to experience music, as of being prepared to pay to get away from it. Music has become part of the noise system that surrounds our lives like air. It is indeed constantly on the air and in the air: it assails us at home, in the factory, at the restaurant; and there are commercial firms who make a living recommending the right kind of background music to anyone who may ask – be he manager of a shop for selling expensive gowns, or a dentist or an undertaker.

All this means that there is a strong temptation today to under-value music, to take it for granted. Even thirty years ago the composer and conductor Constant Lambert wrote a book in which he complained of 'the appalling popularity of music'. Moreover, the persistent absorption of music by the ear and mind cannot be without effect. One recalls the subliminal advertising which consists of throwing messages on to the cinema or television screen for such a short space of time that the mind does not consciously identify and record their meaning, but they are received by the sub-conscious mind and are thereby able to influence the watcher. We may not listen to the background music, we may not consciously take it in, but it is likely to affect our musical values, and maybe even our ability to appreciate other music.

In this connexion the phenomenon of 'Music While You Work' is worth attention. Those who arrange music for this BBC programme have to keep the music completely simple; a too original and unusual touch in the arrangement, like a counter-melody set off against the main tune, might attract attention and distract the worker's mind from the essential objective, which is the carrying out of his or her individual task. If you have to perform a dull repetitive mechanical act throughout the working day it may well be that you will be thankful for a background noise of musical sounds; it may also be quite possible that your productivity will be greater because of it; but it is equally clear that by the very nature of things you are constantly absorbing music passively like a sponge, and you are having to make no conscious effort, mental or otherwise, to increase your comprehension of the music;

indeed, it is specially designed to make such effort of comprehension unnecessary.

Such music is intended simply as a background. You may like to have it on the car radio to while away a long journey. It quite openly sets out to act as a kind of drug which soothes the mind and softens the sub-conscious, but does not stimulate the attentive mind.

When one begins to think a little more about this music, a rather surprising fact emerges. One would have expected that the 'soft lights and sweet music' would be the prevailing mood; and it comes as something of a shock to realize that, since the basic repertoire of this background music is the 'Top Twenty', slowly sentimental numbers are no more common than the strong 'beat' music of the rock groups. Only the other day I had my hair cut to the accompaniment of a lively 'twist' number; and the quiet rhythm of the cutters was in no way disturbed.

Yet this very same music, played at maximum volume in a youth club, would encourage a lively jiving session and a general atmosphere of exuberant vitality.

Can it be that the effect of the music is to a large extent governed by its volume; that its actual content – melodies, harmonies, rhythms – are less important than the mere fact of existence? Played loudly and blatantly it excites; played softly and unobtrusively it soothes. Its intrinsic character matters little. 'I Can't Help Falling in Love' played fortissimo stings more than 'Let's Twist Again' toned down to below conversation level.

This somewhat surprising conclusion suggests that there is nothing inherently different between one 'pop' tune and another – nothing essential in the music itself which belongs either to real emotion or to an inner unmistakable vitality. To make a comparison with classical music, one cannot conceive of Chopin's Funeral March over-blown into sonorous amplified raucousness; sadness and softness are of the essence of the music. And the first movement of Beethoven's Fifth Symphony is based on an impelling rhythm which makes nonsense of any attempt to reduce it to background music. Those who like

music as a background to other activities are right to reject
Beethoven's music; it does not fit into the category.

2

Let us trace some of the origins of modern popular music.

Over the years there have developed two different traditions
in music. One is what we call 'art music', or (wrongly) classical
music. In this the composer puts down his ideas on paper as exactly as possible, and the duty of the performer is to give as
accurate an interpretation as he can of what the composer
wrote, playing the 'correct' notes in the 'correct' time.

On the other hand, there is a tradition of popular music, or,
as it is more commonly called, folk music, which has somewhat
different characteristics. First of all, and fundamentally, the
popular music tradition is an aural one. Tunes are handed
down from one singer to another, and often change in the process. A singer may take liberties with a tune, may alter the
notes or the rhythm, may purposely attack a note below pitch
(as blues singers often do). There are some accepted common
habits of performance, and an instrumentalist will harmonize
a tune by ear with certain conventional and well-worn patterns
of chords.

The two traditions have not always been as far apart and as
clearly differentiated as they are today. It is of course only
since music began to be written down in accurate notation that
the extended compositions of the classical writers have been
possible; and even up to the time of Handel and Mozart in
the eighteenth century a good deal of improvisation took place
in the performance of art music. But, as time went on, the two
streams diverged more sharply. As every aspect of life became
more prone to specialization, the composer of art music became more and more a professional writing for an educated
audience, mainly aristocratic or middle-class, and more out of
touch with the peasant or factory worker. In England, the folk
tradition itself lost a great deal of its hold on everyday life because the old communities were broken up and destroyed by

the Industrial Revolution; and it was only about 1900 that Cecil Sharp and others began to collect and to attempt to breathe a new life into the old folk-songs and dances. But while we owe them an incalculable debt for rescuing a great many lovely tunes which might otherwise have been lost, they did not always sufficiently realize that the old order in which this music had flourished had changed, and that much of it was irrelevant to a new society.

It was about the same time as this that jazz was making its first appearance in and around New Orleans. Many influences went to the making of jazz; but nearly all of them stemmed from the popular tradition – the Negro's songs of oppression, the dances of the Spaniards, and the African rhythms brought via the West Indians. Only the brass band music could be called partially an influence from the tradition of Western written music; and indeed the regular four-in-a-bar underlying pulse and the simple harmonic structures of the band marches were among the most important European elements in jazz. But it was by borrowing these and using them in the context of the popular tradition, with a great deal of improvisation, that the early jazz performers developed their characteristic music.

Jazz, in its traditional form at least, is true folk music. It has all the qualities listed above as typical of folk music and distinct from art music; and it is well known that many traditional players – not merely the amateurs – cannot read music.

It is true that in its modern style jazz is much less of a spontaneous improvised music. Controversy reigns as to whether commercial-style, big band music is true jazz; purists are commonly scathing about the claims of compositions like Gershwin's 'Rhapsody in Blue' to be considered jazz, and the intellectual and somewhat grandiose conceptions in which modernists such as Stan Kenton imitate some of the contemporary composers like Stravinsky are even more uncertainly designated as jazz.

Nevertheless no living means of artistic expression stands still. There is always development, and inevitably the original form of free-and-easy traditional jazz has been followed by

156

many changes, most of which have been in the direction either of a larger grouping of instrumentalists or of more complex and sophisticated harmonies – both of which lead away from the true popular style and demand written arrangements and trained, rehearsed musicians.

Yet at the same time it is true that, whether it be mainstream or modern, or just plain commercial, you can usually trace the origin of each number to one or other of the two basic traditional jazz forms – the blues, with its lazy, dragging rhythm, its set harmonic structure and its characteristic nostalgic note of oppression or of the frustrated search for the unattainable; or alternatively the high-spirited, noisy brashness of the four-in-a-bar quickstep rhythm, deriving from the old band marches, enlivened by the syncopating improvisations of generations of Negro jazz musicians.

Thus the development of jazz as seen in the big bands of Duke Ellington and the commercial swing combinations of the thirties, and equally by the small 'chamber' groups, is natural and proper. Many may still prefer the spontaneity and the uninhibitedness of traditional jazz, with its simple sequences of well-used chords and its insistence on improvisation by the melody instruments; but this is not to deny to the other manifestations the name of jazz. No one can listen to the Modern Jazz Quartet or the Dave Brubeck Quartet, for example, without realizing that the music has in it the essence of the jazz spirit. In both groups the drummer will create just that beat, whether it be the relaxed withheld swing of the slow blues tempo, or the exciting onward thrust of the quick movements, which is one of the hallmarks of good jazz. The curious and fascinating combinations of sound which both quartets derive from their choice of instruments may be far removed from the unsophisticated trumpet, clarinet, or saxophone; and the chord progressions may contain a good deal of the chromatic harmonies of the late nineteenth century art music and be less instinctive and more worked out. But the quality and spirit are undeniably the quality and spirit of jazz.

But there is one particular feature of the original jazz which is of special interest to us. Because this music belongs to the tradition of music handed down aurally, music which is not put into permanent written form before performance, its underlying pattern must be basically simple. Thus, we have the blues form with its established formula of a twelve-bar sequence of chords. The strict blues always keeps to this same pattern of chords; it is a most restricted form, and it is amazing how much variety has been obtained within it. It is a formula which is ideal for its purposes of aurally improvised music. Every singer and performer knows the harmonic pattern and feels it instinctively through long familiarity; thus they can improvise freely within the framework. On the other hand, the rigidity of the scheme makes it unsuitable for large-scale development. It is not surprising that no one has ever written a successful 'blues' symphony. 'Rhapsody in Blue' does not use the normal blues formula, and in any case its great weakness is its scrappiness, its lack of cohesion. It is equally true that few of the art composers of the written tradition have successfully produced large-scale compositions using folk melodies. Once again we see that the essential characteristics of folk and popular music are spontaneity and immediacy, as opposed to the long span of most art music, where one of the most important things is to be able to remember what happened two or three minutes ago, and to relate it to what you are hearing now.

It is the same with the 'quickstep' numbers, as I have rather arbitrarily chosen to call them. Take an old favourite like 'Alexander's Ragtime Band', and note how on a recording by the traditional New Orleans team led by Bunk Johnson the number consists of seven or eight variations improvised over the basic harmonic pattern of the tune – no development occurs, and no contrasting material is introduced; the formula is as simple as that of the blues, and as appropriate for the purpose.

I have emphasized this aspect of the essential simplicity of form of all traditional and most other jazz because it has an important bearing on the commercial popular music – the 'pop' music – which to a large extent has grown from it. Let us now turn to a further consideration of this music.

3

We have seen how, in the normal order of things, jazz has developed and changed through the demands of the society in which it existed. The commercial values of white American society and the need for an easy, not too intellectual communal recreation for the population of their great cities led to the creation of a vast entertainment industry which utilized the new Negro music for its own purpose. This industry was able to make use of men like Duke Ellington and Benny Goodman, but inevitably the music they provided altered in character from the old-style jazz.

The period between the wars saw the greatest growth of modern ballroom dance music; and there was a strong connexion between jazz and this music. While the purist will express disgust at the failure of the uninitiated to distinguish between 'jazz' and 'dance' music, yet it cannot be denied that a great deal of ballroom music since the twenties has taken most of its character from jazz influences. The role of the drummer, holding together the melody instruments through his pervasive beat, and assisted by bass and other members of the rhythm section, is a direct parallel; and the instrumentation, with its emphasis on brass, saxophones, and drums, stems similarly from jazz. Furthermore, with the exception of the waltz, which has triumphantly maintained its place in ballrooms for well over a hundred years, and the introduction of Latin-American rhythms – some of which in any case were in at the beginning of jazz – the two main ingredients of modern dance music are again the quickstep and the slow four-in-a-bar quasi-blues.

But a third element has appeared and, more particularly during the past twenty or so years, has radically altered the face of popular music. This is the enormous diffusion of music through the mass media, and notably the gramophone. And it is with this that we are particularly concerned here.

It is of course only the existence of records and radio that has enabled jazz to sweep the world in a way that it has done.

But for these aids to dissemination it would doubtless have remained a localized folk music native to the Southern States of its origin. It would have spread to Chicago and those northern towns where Negroes had settled in considerable numbers, and might have attained some popularity among local whites. But it would no more have become a common interest of millions throughout the world than have the polkas and dumkas of Bohemia, or the scottisches and reels of the Highlands. The fortunate circumstance was that an exciting and upspringing new music grew up in a country which was first to adapt itself to mass production and which had the opportunity of wide diffusion which came from the growth of mechanical reproduction.

There are a few people who deplore the fact that jazz has had such popularity thrust upon it through the workings of commercial enterprise. Now, quite apart from the fact that without its aid many of such critics might themselves barely have heard of jazz, it is surely unreasonable to complain because so many people in so many countries have been enabled to enjoy a new experience.

Yet the inevitable effects of mass reproduction of music, and particularly of folk music, are not all good. We have seen that one of the chief features of folk music is its spontaneity, its immediacy. If, on the spur of the moment, a folk musician feels like altering the tune, or improvising, he is entitled to do so. Like the comedian in pantomime, he is allowed and even expected to gag. The music is intimate, and a folk singer is in his element when performing to a small group of his associates, in intimate surroundings; there is a direct *rapport* between him and his audience, which derives from the fact that they belong to a common society and enjoy a common inheritance.

Now these conditions are the precise opposite to those of commercial recording. What is wanted here is something which will appeal to a vast international audience; what by the nature of things has to be put on disc is something fixed and unchangeable; direct contact and mutual sparking off of enthusiasms between performers and listeners is impossible.

All this might suggest that pure traditional jazz, along with other folk music, is the most unsuitable type of music for recording purposes. And indeed this is to a large extent true. Not only trad, but also all other comparable forms of improvisatory music, like skiffle, are best enjoyed 'off the cuff' when you join with a crowd of enthusiasts like yourself at the jazz club or the coffee bar, and the music itself lights up from the environment, and the players are possessed by the occasion.

It is of course true that some of the best records, not only of jazz, but also of classical music, have been made under conditions of normal public performance. But the technique of the recording studio itself is utterly removed from spontaneity. Takes and re-takes continue until a performance is passed as perfect; and the final issued version may be a synthetic construction from a number of performances joined together by tape and scissors as a film is cut and patched.

Inevitably this affects the style of the music recorded. If a number is to be rehearsed several times, and if the eventual result is going to be placed on permanent record, there is every reason for sticking to a written arrangement, and limiting improvisation as much as possible. And if a record needs to sell tens of thousands of copies and have an international market, it is natural to attempt to produce what is known to be acceptable and popular.

Record companies thus find themselves in the position of every operator of a mass medium of communication, which the Pilkington Committee on broadcasting so well described when they said that the programmes provided and viewed by millions are not necessarily the most popular in that they are everybody's, or indeed anybody's first choice; but they are tolerated enough to be accepted by more viewers than any alternative. Such alternative might be more eagerly awaited and enjoyed by many, but would not be accepted by others, who in their turn would have their own positive first preferences. A middle-of-the-road mediocrity, offending no one, is the inevitable result.

It is a tribute to the vitality of jazz that it has so well survived this natural tendency of the commercial world to bring everything to a common measure and eliminate the individual element. Yet it has not escaped unscathed, and as true jazz shades off into dance music and pop, the role of the stereotyped and conventional gets steadily greater, and finally the spontaneous creativeness of folk music has no place.

Yet pop music has arisen to meet a genuine demand.

Folk music in the traditional sense – music played or sung round the village green, music used to accompany ceremonials like harvesting – belongs to the small community as exemplified in the English village of pre-industrial times. The art music of the written tradition is too the music of a community, but of a very different kind. It stems from a leisured class or group, a group that has time and learning to write down its music, and to rehearse complex and difficult works. Originally this community was pre-eminently the church; after the Middle Ages it became more and more the courts of the secular nobility of Europe. As recently as the late eighteenth century Haydn and Mozart wrote most of their music for performance in the salon of some wealthy patron. These princes had their own private orchestras and theatres, and hence the classical composers developed their orchestral symphonies, their chamber music and operas.

During the great nineteenth century transition from an aristocratic and mainly agricultural society to the industrial age in which we live now men and women were herded into the factories and slums; and the indigenous popular music and dancing began to die out. At the other end of the scale the music of the art musicians began to be enjoyed by a wider social class, and composers such as Mendelssohn wrote for the middle class Victorian drawing-room.

In the barren and bleak environment of the nineteenth century industrial town, however, nothing very notable in the way of a new people's music flourished. There were the music-hall songs, and this was indeed a popular music in a limited way; but it was not until the growth of jazz and of the dance music developed from it that the urban masses began to find something which had a special appeal.

And so it was at this point that everything came together. The new kind of music; the means of disseminating it widely through the gramophone and, later, the radio; the commercial world of mass production for profit; and the new twentieth century folk – people with little experience either in self-expression in music or the arts or of any sort of cultural background, but people with a steadily increasing amount of money and leisure. Some form of release through music they sought, as every human community has sought it; and some form they were given.

So developed the new industry, an industry for the provision of popular music. As Christian Darnton has said, folk music (as commonly understood) is 'music which comes from the people', whereas popular music (again as commonly understood) is 'music written *for* the people'; and the achievement of the business interests in Tin Pan Alley and the recording companies has been to manufacture a music for the people on the largest possible scale. They have done this, as such things must be done, by a process of standardization, by providing an article which will be accepted by most of the people most of the time.

4

Let us look at the content of an average Top Twenty hit and see why it is cast in the particular mould which we all know so well.

A good deal has been written about the lyrics of pop songs. Partly this is because it is always easier to write about words than about music; nevertheless, the lines to which the top tunes are set are in themselves revealing.

Obviously the theme must be relevant – that is to say, it must be 'about' one of the universal themes which appeal to all. Of these, the girl–boy motif is the surest winner, more especially since the growth of the teen-age market has led to a special assault on that section of the community. In earlier decades other themes have had a long run for their money; the local state-love of the American led to a whole era of songs praising Wyoming, Alabama, Mississippi, Omaha; Hawaiian islands and coal-black mammies have also had their turn. But nowadays more than ever the love theme is almost universal in commercial lyrics.

But, as has been frequently pointed out, it must be love of a very romantic and sentimental nature. In the twenties they sang

We'll have a blue room, a new room, for two room,
Where every day's a holiday, because you're married to me.

Today it is

Come outside, there's a lovely moon out there,
Come outside while we've got time to spare.

There may occasionally be the lyric of the frustrated lover, but it is never the frustration of everyday human circumstance ; always the singer and the object of his or her song inhabit a dream world, seated as it were on remote clouds of insubstantial candy-floss, with nothing to think about but their romantic emotions.

In this respect there is a great difference between the real folk jazz and the pop. The blues singers did not tell of an idealized world but of a very real one where pain and trouble were common experiences – where music and song might help you to overcome trouble but not by pretending it didn't exist. Jazz has been called a music of protest ; and in so far as it came from a slave people, a racially oppressed people, it was just this. In this lay some of its appeal to the industrialized city dwellers, who themselves knew what oppression meant, and who felt the heartache of the blues.

Now it's ashes to ashes, sweet papa, dust to dust,
I said ashes to ashes, I mean dust to dust :
Now show me the man any woman can trust.

Without trying to draw too rigid a dividing-line between one type and another, and remembering that, as we have seen, there is an infinite variety ranging from the purest folk-jazz to the most manufactured pop song, it remains that one of the surest marks of the non-commercial can be seen in the integrity of the lyric – how far it mirrors a real world rather than the imitation of

> I remember you,
> You're the one who made my dreams come true.

Inside the field of the commercial pop this is the typical pattern; even defenders of the species will usually admit the crushing banality of the lyrics, and one normally has to go outside the world of the Top Twenty to find genuine ideas. A mere scanning of the titles or opening lines of the hit parade at any given time will indicate this:

> Dream, dream, baby;
> Dream, dream, baby;
>> How long must I dream?
> Dream, dream, baby;
>> You can make my dreams come true.

> I can't stop loving you

> Roses are red, my love,
> Violets are blue;
> Sugar is sweet, my love,
> But not as sweet as you.

One and all, these refer to the world where June rhymes with moon, where there is no such thing as struggle for existence, where love does not have to be striven for through understanding. Even the ballads of unrequited love are basically of the same material.

> They say I'll love again some day,
> True love will come my way
>> The next time.
> But after you there'll never be
>> A next time
>> For me.

There is still the one theme, emptied of content, reduced to a formula.

But songs with a different, and stronger, note can be popular, though they may not reach the charts.

> Where have all the flowers gone,
>> Long time passing,

165

> Where have all the flowers gone,
>   Long time ago?
> Where have all the flowers gone?
>   Young girls picked them everyone.
>   When will they ever learn?
>
> Where have all the young girls gone, etc ...
>   Gone to young men everyone.
>
> Where have all the young men gone, etc ...
>   Gone to soldiers everyone.
>
> Where have all the soldiers gone, etc ...
>   Gone to graveyards everyone.
>
> Where have all the graveyards gone, etc ...
>   Gone to flowers everyone.
>   When will they ever learn?

Yet without moving from the more exclusively pop world itself the more academic minds among us may learn some lessons – in particular, that though one must often flinch at the banality of the conventionalized romance, one may sometimes come across a directness of speech and a piquancy of phrase which make the vernacular a medium for poetry. If an adolescent is made to sing at school

> Youth's the season made for joys,
> Love is then our duty

it is not altogether surprising that he turns with pleasurable relief to Cliff Richard:

> You are a stick of dynamite
> Sitting on a coffee bar stool.

It is rarely, however, that this spirit of delight comes to the commercial pop.

But of course any art must be about and must grow from one's own existence, one's own emotion and living; and if the words and sentiment are expressed with a banality and a superficiality, it may be because the background and the environment and the education of most of us twentieth century common men have not yet given us the ability to be more articulate about our loves and lives.

5

What about the music of pops? We must consider, first, the actual form of the music, and, secondly, its content and quality.

Just as the words take a basic, universal theme, denude it of any real individuality of utterance, and serve it up for mass commercial consumption, so the music is standardized to a pattern. It is stated that an electronic brain has been invented which can 'compose' melodies; and there would seem no logical reason why in fact a robot machine could not produce at least a passable imitation of a pop tune.

The hit tune, let us remember, derives from the popular aural tradition of music. It owes little to the written tradition by which a musical theme is 'developed' and grows from one moment to the next. The folk tune is immediate and direct; and because it has to be remembered complete by those who reproduce it, it must be essentially simple in shape and form.

We have noted how the simple pattern of the blues enables the performers to improvise freely and easily. The form of the march and of many short instrumental melodies is frequently a thirty-two bar sequence; and this is used for most quick dance-tunes. This frame consists of four sections of eight bars each, of which the first and last are usually the same, and the second is a repetition with only a very slight variation of the first. The pop industry has taken over this formula as an almost universal standardized pattern. But whereas such a simple design is not only acceptable but necessary as a background for improvisation, its constant repetition as the basis of a once-for-all composed lyric and melody can barely avoid monotony, and today has reached the stage of what Francis Newton calls 'assembly line' composition.

Thus the pop music world has taken an elementary formula which is admirable for such purposes as folk dance music or collective improvisations, and has used it for pre-composed numbers so that originality in composition has the least possible opportunity, while at the same time not much place is left in the modern commercial recording process for spontaneous creation during performance.

Nevertheless, because of the importance of the performer in all popular music, it is particularly difficult to make any worth while value judgements on paper. Most musicians know well the experience of having heard some great popular artist – Paul Robeson is the supreme example – who has taken a song which on the cold bare music paper appears to be empty and banal, and who has by combination of artistry and complete sincerity made a vital human message out of the music.

In any case, the actual appearance of the notes on paper is not the criterion of value of a piece of music in the aural tradition, since it is precisely in the departure from the written score that much of its character lies.

If a record is to sell as near as maybe a million copies, the tune must be something which appeals instantly to as many as possible. Now, with the greatest melodies of the world, whether classical or folk, one can often say that when you have heard them you feel that they could not have been otherwise, that each note as it is played or sung seems to follow inevitably from the one before; yet the greatness of the tune and its composer lies precisely in the fact that none of us could ourselves have imagined that melody if we had never heard it before, not even if we had been given the first phrase. But a melody like that may take a hearing or two to make its full appeal; the tune for the Top Twenty must take at once, and to do this it is necessary that from the start it shall follow the expected path. Given the opening phrase, any average composer could finish the tune and the result would be very much what is eventually published.

As a general principle, the fewer gimmicks, the easier it is for a genuine musical quality to show through. In a record like Chris Montez' 'Let's Dance' the repetitive rhythm, the over-amplification of the guitars and the triteness of the melody are not compensated for by a high-spirited performance. On the other hand, in any hit selection at the present day there will be a number of straightforward tunes, with nothing very original about them, tied as firmly to the three or four primary chords of classical harmony as much as any theme of Beethoven's; but if these numbers are presented with a minimum of affectation by an artist whose human voice is allowed to come through, they can give an honest musical pleasure. One thinks, at the time of writing, of 'Bachelor Boy', 'Bobby's Girl', or 'Swiss Maid'. Though none is likely to remain in currency for years, as a few outstanding numbers have done, they meet satisfactorily the needs of modern popular musical culture.

If not much originality can be expected from the tune, this throws a considerable responsibility on the arranger; and indeed the arrangement is often a key factor in the success or otherwise of a commercial number.

The arrangers (who, true to the specialization which is a mark of modern industry, are not the same people as the tune-writers) are not infrequently musicians of some skill. A tune which may be no better than its fellows may be lifted out of the ordinary by a backing in which there is an accompanying rhythm of character (good use nowadays is being made of the familiar calypso rhythm), or in which use is made of the instruments to play counter-melodies to the vocal line. Yet too often the arrangers are content to draw on other forms of music and create from them a stereotyped pattern, which can be used over and over again for different songs so long as the fashion for that type remains, after which a new formula is borrowed.

This is best illustrated by the fate of skiffle music.

For many years the hit tunes were usually straightforward dance band melodies – a fox-trot or a waltz, or perhaps a Latin-American rhythm. Occasionally a sentimental ballad number might have a turn, or a song hit from a show, like 'Old Man River' or 'The Lambeth Walk'. Then came the gradual spread of interest in other types of American folk song – the hillbilly, the 'country and western', the music of Burl Ives and Josh White. Suddenly the teen-age world was hit by skiffle. Boys discovered the fascination of a new easy-going form of spontaneous music-making in which the principal elements were guitars used as rhythmic and harmonic background to folky melodies ranging from spirituals and blues to cowboy songs. It was easier to play and sing skiffle than jazz; and it

169

required none of the formal knowledge of written music. It became almost in a matter of weeks an occupation for thousands of performers and many more of their followers.

What was the reaction of the commercial world? At once they saw that here was a perfect vehicle for the mass recording process. Lyrics which 'belonged', basically simple but rhythmic tunes, and a set type of instrumental accompaniment. All that was needed was to 'hot up' the style, to amplify the guitars (the electric guitar is not just a different instrument from the orthodox variety, it is a much inferior one), to make full use of echo chambers and the rest of the recording gimmicks, and to find one or two recording artists of the right kind.

So popular has this style become that nearly every Top Ten hit today has as its main instrumental backing the amplified guitar and rhythm section which derives from skiffle music – whether it is in the mood of rock-and-roll or more relaxed and romantic. But in order to reach the largest public with the least expenditure the style has been vulgarized and stereotyped to a degree where most of its original creativeness has been driven out.

6

We come now to the performer, the recording artist.

In folk music proper the performer is important because of his direct creative contribution. An enthusiast looks on the label of a jazz record not for the composer of a piece, but for the performers. In pops the performer's personality is important, but for a rather different reason. For the number to take, the record-buyer must be able to identify himself with it; just as the theme must be one of the universals, so the singer should be an ordinary chap – one of us. The teen-age idol need bring no very great musical or technical skill to his work; but he must attract the fans, and they must be able to feel that the romantic idealized world in which he lives (in public) is one which they, Walter Mitty-like, may too inhabit.

An excellent idea of the way in which the modern publicity machine builds up the chosen artist in order to project him to the world may be gained by reading the very frank description of the launching of Tommy Steele given by his manager, John Kennedy. Gimmicks, deliberate inventions (which some people would call 'lies') and constant expenditure to keep the star in public view are all part of the tactics. With the best of them, like Steele himself, their own character and personality may carry them beyond a merely ephemeral fame; the majority do not survive their promoter's favour, and are dependent on the publicity process for such success as they attain. This identification of the listener of himself with the star – or, more accurately, with the object of the star's attentions, since most of the fans of the boy singers are girls – is the most convincing proof of the escapist nature of this world. Its function is to present an ideal synthetic dream picture, which is far removed from the function of true art, which holds up a mirror to the real world.

It would seem therefore a not unfair verdict on the commercial pop industry of today that it has not invented or created anything fundamentally new. It has borrowed rhythms and formulae from jazz; it has borrowed from skiffle and white American folk music; it has taken many harmonies and instrumental colourings from Western art music; and what it has borrowed it has reduced to a mechanical process. Yet it has filled a gap; as Charles Parker has said, there is a 'genuine human need for some place of refuge, some fantasy world where the inadequacies of the actual world can be challenged and – at least vicariously – redressed'.

The discriminating music-lover should look beyond the pops back to their origins – to the truly popular or people's music which grew as a direct response to the need of everyman for expression of his feelings, loves, sorrows, and cares. He may then see jazz, particularly the traditional variety, as a music coming straight from the hearts and minds of the Negro people. He may also be moved to look further at the skiffle movement, and see that, while the majority of skiffle enthusiasts have followed the record companies into the rock and post-rock era, a very considerable number have developed an interest in the modern folk music world of Alan Lomax and Pete Seeger, of Ewan MacColl and Joe Gordon, of the folk music clubs where not only do young people hear and join in the ballads and choruses of today but where new songs are still being made through the natural creative process which over the ages has turned our desires and feelings into songs.

Thus the gap which popular recorded music fills is the gap between, on the one hand, the art music of a leisured, mainly upper-class society, and, on the other, the folk music of a people who because of their surge into industrialism and modern city life have lost touch with their folkways. But the vast enthusiasm for the do-it-yourself music of skiffle and 'trad' jazz and the new folk music clubs which are springing up in every city suggests that many young people are finding the gap more satisfactorily filled by a return to something like the old spontaneous tradition. In this process the influence of American-style music is bound to be considerable, because it has been the first music of its kind to receive universal dissemination. But the value of other popular cultural heritages will become increasingly apparent.

7

Does this mean then that the great record industry has after all nothing of value to offer? That we should all be much better off without it, making our own amateur and amateurish music in our own back yards?

Clearly not; one need only look back to the picture of fifty years ago painted at the beginning of this chapter. It may be easy to undervalue music today, but no one willingly exchanges the plenty of the promised land for the privation of the desert. What the gramophone provides to a degree that nothing else can remotely approach is the opportunity of choice. Practically all worthwhile music, as well as much of little value, is obtainable today on disc; and each of us can sample for himself the offered wares – pops, jazz, light and classical, old and modern. We can take what we want and leave the rest. Our musical world today has been made an affluent society beyond the dreams of our fathers.

But the element of choice involves necessarily the need for

discrimination. No one can assimilate everything that is available; everyone has to choose. The best value is obtained by the one who ranges widely and samples much, and who has some sound basis for value-judgements as between one article and another. This basis comes from some knowledge of the background and from attention to and awareness of the subject matter – in this case the music – such as background listening cannot provide.

Here we have endeavoured to sketch a background to the popular side of recorded music. But it would be unreal not to look for at least a moment at recorded music as a whole. 'I remember you' may have sold 102,500 copies in one day, and a quarter of a million may be a fair average for a winner in the Top Ten stakes; but there are numerous listed recordings of Beethoven's Fifth Symphony; and a popularly-priced disc of one version only of such a major classic may sell between 20,000 and 50,000 copies, most of which will be listened to long after the pop tune has been dismissed. Moreover, the sales of classical records, including such lighter music as Gilbert and Sullivan, amount to about twenty per cent of the total, which is over twice as much as the score of jazz.

So, while the main purpose of this chapter has been to show how the mass-produced pop has grown to its present shape and size, we should, to see the subject in perspective, appreciate that the greatest debt that we owe to the recording companies derives from the infinite variety of their catalogues. Every possible wish is catered for; and it is precisely this plethora of records offered which makes the value and the rewards of discriminating choice so great.

After all, it is a complete illusion, to which few readers would surely subscribe, that art and classical music on the one hand and jazz and pops on the other are in any way incompatible. They belong indeed to two different traditions of performance, which have tended most unfortunately to grow far apart over the last couple of hundred years. But any normal musical person gets immense satisfaction out of both, and many excellent books exist to help the inexperienced listener in his explorations. Although in general terms the former is more suitable for professional performance to which the amateur listens, while the popular tradition is one of informal amateur performance, modern conditions, and in particular the gramophone, have led to a blurring of this distinction.

One is tempted to go back a little in history, to the Renaissance and its fruits in musical history. The Renaissance, like the twentieth century, was a time when the boundaries of man's knowledge were suddenly and widely extended; new horizons were opened to many of the leisured classes who previously had lived in superstition and ignorance.

Around 1600 a number of cultivated amateurs in Italy came together with the object of reviving the old Greek drama which the new learning had revealed. They hoped themselves to produce works of art on similar lines. What they did create was, not restored Greek drama, but a new music. They composed the first operas, and they established new patterns of musical form and new techniques of musical expression which paved the way for the whole amazing flowering of European art music from that time – the operas and oratorios of Handel, the symphonies and quartets of Mozart and Haydn and Beethoven, the great romantic music of the nineteenth century, of Schubert and Wagner, Dvorak and Tschaikowsky.

Maybe we are today on the verge of a new Renaissance. But today it is not only the leisured aristocracy who have the new knowledge at their disposal; it is everyman. A new music in the twentieth century will not come from the professional composer or the intellectual music-lover alone; it will not come from jazz alone, because too much of the essential meaning of jazz belongs to the American Negro alone. It will not be the product of a mass medium of communication, but these will help immeasurably to propagate it; it may well owe much to the folk revival of the last ten years, particularly if trained musicians and teachers understand sympathetically the roots and social meaning of this revival. But ultimately it will grow only if new generations continue to see and use music as more than a background, more than a business, as a personal expression of all that they themselves feel most deeply and believe in most fully.

BOOKS

N. HENTOFF AND N. SHAPIRO, *ed., Hear Me Talkin' to Ya* (Penguin). Jazz men talking informally about their music and background.

DONALD HUGHES, *Let's Have Some Music* (Museum Press). Attempts to bring all kinds of music under one cover; written for teen-agers.

JOHN KENNEDY, *Tommy Steele* (Souvenir Press). Kennedy was Steele's manager. A frank and entertaining book.

A. L. LLOYD, *The Singing Englishman* (Workers' Music Association). The English folk-song story from an unusual but challenging angle.

J. AND A. LOMAX, *American Ballads and Folk Songs* (The Macmillan Co.). Includes many of the now widely known American traditional songs.

REGINALD NETTEL, *The Englishman Makes Music* (Phoenix). Some account of the social background of English musical life.

FRANCIS NEWTON, *The Jazz Scene* (Penguin). The best introduction to jazz.

MARSHALL STEARNS, *The Story of Jazz* (Sidgwick and Jackson). A fuller history, and a very readable one, of the development of jazz.

FOOTNOTE

The ephemeral nature of pop music means that many of the numbers quoted in this article may be unknown by the time it is in the hands of the reader. Even the Beatle phenomenon lay in the future at the time of writing; it is perhaps worth a footnote.

Everything in the Beatle story illustrates the main thesis we have put forward. The group began in an atmosphere of combined rock and folk – the post-skiffle era. They are sufficiently close to the true popular tradition to write their own songs, and this is one of the secrets of their success, for there is at times, particularly in some of their earlier numbers, an individual quality which is fresher and less synthetic than the output of the normal assembly-line. To this has been added an outstanding managerial skill and a gimmickry. This combination of genuine creative ability in the popular idiom (liable, unfortunately, to be increasingly crushed out of existence as time goes on) with modern mass salesmanship techniques has led to their success. Incidentally, it is doubtful whether the emotional crises which many young women suffer at the sight of the modern pop star has been paralleled since the young pianist Franz Liszt – who also had a distinctive hair-style – burst upon the astonished middle-class concert-goers over a hundred years ago.

MICHAEL FARR

We live in a designed world. Design determines the function
and shape of streets and buildings, of cars and clothes. In all
man-made things it is a conditioning force from the Stone Age
axe to the space ship. Nothing can be made or used without a
'design', whether it be crude or subtle. The fact that there is
a design behind everything artificial means that any discussion
of it as such would be too generalized to have any value in a
short essay. Here we are concerned with consumer goods,
those articles which are made for use in and around the home.

Pay a visit to any friends' house and see how they live in it.
Observe their movements in carrying out simple tasks; don't
comment, just observe and you will be amazed by the amount
of conflict between them and their equipment. The preparation of a meal would be a suitable – and typical – object for
study. There will be a lot of bending, stretching, and hunting
for the necessary tools and containers. Could the cupboards
and drawers which house them be more conveniently designed? Could the tools themselves, can-openers, cookery
books, knives, and grill pans be more efficient and safe to use?
Is the working top the right height for comfort, the lighting
placed where it can be most effective, the cooker with its boil-
ing fat and scalding liquids proof from the prying hands of
children?

This list of questions would only be the beginning of a wide-
ranging and profound inquiry which has not yet been made,
because of apathy on the part of manufacturers and adapt-
ability on the part of the users, most of whom are cursed with
a stoic streak that enables them to 'make do' and 'muddle
through' with whatever equipment they have been able to find
and afford.

As our civilization is maintained and steadily 'improved' by the profits of mass-producing industry, so it must live with the system's so-called 'end-products'. One design of end-product must suit 10,000 human beings; so runs the equation determined least by the individual needs of the user and most by the cost of machine tools, assembly-line production, distribution, and advertising budgets.

It is clear that the commercial success of a mass-produced article is not necessarily a true indication of its usefulness to the consumer. Often it is purchased only because it is the best of its kind or the cheapest on the market. Is this inevitable or can some form of research be maintained to provide designers and manufacturers with information on the individual consumer's real needs and preferences? First, let us see the problem in its context by outlining current methods of producing and selling.

From the inception of a design in the form of rough sketches, general statistics and verbal opinions to the stage when it reaches the market, there is a long chain of failures and achievements. These gradually build up as a series of decisions, which give the final product its essential characteristics expressed in function, shape, colour, and price. The design is then passed by the company's sales staff to wholesalers and so to retailers who sell it to the customer. It is then used. In its development stages a design – say it is a clothes-washer – is affected by persons in the factory whose demands must be recognized and, if necessary, finally met by a series of compromises. The washing machine will often have at all stages the guiding hand of its initiator, the designer, yet the others will exert their specialized influences: the managing director himself, the development and production engineers, the foremen of production, packing, and warehousing, leading to the managers of sales, advertising, and publicity. All these individuals will know – with a degree of certainty that gains strength with age – what they expect the washing machine to be and how it should behave for them. Yet, in very many cases they do not look upon it as something which is to become an essential part of someone else's life.

A washing machine is used as an example here as we are concerned with mass-production designs: radios, plates, cutlery, chairs, refrigerators, motor cars, and so on. In quantities ranging between 5,000 and 50,000 they are produced, each one identical with the next, each having been subject to the requirements of a mere handful of people at the factory and distribution stages. The consumer takes over when the design's every shape and movement have been agreed. In what way can the design satisfy the user's own particular but important demands? He has bought the design for his home but to what extent has it been suited to his home?

The problem here concerns communications and a brief digression will help to bring it into focus. Under a different social order, such as that which prevailed in the eighteenth century, the majority of designs for domestic use were produced by individual craftsmen for one customer at a time. Within the craftsman's understanding of the contemporary idiom or style there was scope for appreciating and meeting the user's real needs. The workshop system in towns and villages throughout the country was a parochial affair, unaffected by problems of distribution and distance. During the inception and execution of the design the two parties, craftsman and user, made their contribution to ensure that the result suited them both.

This state of affairs is clearly recalled by George Sturt in *The Wheelwright's Shop*:

I only know that in these and a hundred details every well-built farm-waggon (of whatever variety) was like an organism, reflecting in every curve and dimension some special need of its own countryside.... They were so exact. Just as a biologist may see, in any limpet, signs of the rocky shore, the smashing breakers, so the provincial wheelwright could hardly help reading, from the waggon lines, tales of haymaking and upland fields, of hilly roads and lonely woods. ...

In this rural picture – already a relic when Sturt wrote in 1923 – real satisfaction was achieved by both craftsman and user. Both parties knew each other and could anticipate how each would react. As with farm wagons so with chairs and tables and all other items of equipment in the house. They may have been technologically backward but they were constructed with a conviction and a precision directly derived from the maker's awareness of immediate needs.

Even today most of us can occasionally recapture this *rapprochement* between maker and user. It could follow the order for a bespoke suit, a built-in wardrobe, an engagement ring, or a piece of pottery. In working out the result with the designer or craftsman we can experience a cooperative excitement. The result – the article itself – is usually valued by us more highly than those we bought 'off the peg'. As an aside, it is worth noting that the infrequency with which this is possible probably accounts, in part, for the startling extensions of the 'do-it-yourself' movement in recent years.

But personal contact between maker and user is of course impossible where large quantities of identical items are concerned. We cannot put the clock back. The Industrial Revolution not only blotted out the craft-based systems, it changed the character and aspirations of successive generations. Our lives now are conditioned by the factory system and commercial marketing. The social and economic pressures that have been building themselves up for two centuries are irresistible. Or so it would seem if we were to examine the slender efforts of a few far-sighted individuals who seek a means of coming to terms with the system on human grounds. In contrast we have the attitude of the vast majority who, when not actually earning a living or being buoyed up with promises of bigger and better social advantages just around the corner, escape backwards to inhabit neo-Tudor houses, bother about Beefeaters or trek out to overcrowded stately homes and beauty spots to 'get away from it all'.

The workings of the Industrial Revolution are all too familiar to need re-tracing here. One of its main effects was the division of labour so that no one man dealt with a product from beginning to end. Of greater consequence to us was the way in which it divorced design from execution and in many cases extinguished the designer altogether. From the latter half of the eighteenth century onwards craft-work was progressively mechanized. The intimate contact between men, materials, and the market, which is essential to all creative design, was broken by the intrusion of machines. Standardization of designs led to greater production of cheaper articles. New markets were created where quantity rather than quality was valued for its profitable returns.

After the defeat of the craftsmen the artist turned and fled. In his imagination he was above the mean standards and mechanical methods of the manufacturer. But the public followed the advances of the new industries and forgot the artist, who in turn became progressively separated from the living thoughts and feelings of his time. Throughout the nineteenth century and into the twentieth century the situation got steadily worse. A significant change in attitude had its origin in William Morris who showed, in some of his craftwork, how contemporary vitality could return to manufactured articles by bringing the artist back to the workshop. At a succeeding, but not directly connected stage in this development (which took place largely in Germany between 1905 and 1930) the artist – often in the guise of architect – was persuaded to enter the factory and design articles for quantity production.

Here the concept of 'artist' has important connotations. Although he was performing as a designer he behaved as a being placed apart from the humdrum day-to-day world of industry. He was a person with cultural pretensions called into the industrial scene to give it grace and tone. The majority of independent consultant industrial designers nowadays do not let their privileged position, so recently established, encourage pretentiousness. But the danger is there all the same and manufacturers, the designers' clients, are generally unaware of it. They often call in designers to perform as artists concerned only with the appearance of products, and not also as technically and socially alert consultants who are prepared to work within a team of specialists from the beginning to the end of a product's development programme.

To be fair to the designer in his role of artist it should be said that he has often been a tool in the hands of the propagandists for beauty in industrial products. In the twenties and thirties the campaigning of the Design and Industries Association – although its often repeated slogan has been 'fitness for purpose' – did much to bolster the concept of art in industry. In 1930 the designers' own professional body was founded as the Society of Industrial Artists. Since the war the same attitudes have frequently gained ascendancy. The Council of Industrial Design, started in 1944, and at that time the only official body in the world to tackle the problem, has kept firmly to the term 'design' to describe its work. But even with this organization there has been a tendency to select products for exhibition and publicity primarily because they looked well.

The battle against ugliness in industry and its products has been fought for sixty years, with relevant antecedent campaigns that go much further back. It has been a cause variously taken up by artists, art critics, art historians, architects, designers, manufacturers, retailers, journalists, and government officials. The object of their criticism and cajolery was not simply ugliness, however defined, but such aberrations as machine-made period furniture, 'streamlined' household appliances, fake folk art, and bowdlerizations of high quality modern designs first produced by competitors.

The need to persuade all sections of industry that more imaginative, modern-looking designs are not only possible but desirable should not be questioned: a visit to any department store will show by how far the poor work outweighs the good. The campaign continues, on the platforms of the D.I.A. and in the CoID's Design Centre – a permanent exhibition of modern British design – but the terms of reference are changing. There is now far more concern for functional standards based on what evidence exists to show what users really need. Why has this change in emphasis occurred and how much more profound and definitive can become the information it relies on?

Look at the problem from the manufacturer's point of view. No matter what is said to him by journalists and other critics it is he alone who must decide what designs to put into production to ensure a profitable return to himself and his employees. We have already looked at the chain of persons performing different duties in the factory during the evolution of a design.

They are consumers themselves, it is true, but their own preferences may well not represent those of their potential market. As markets increase and firms prosper, the executives (who take the decisions on what type of design to produce) tend to become remote from their ultimate consumers. They cannot *feel* the needs of people in societies different from their own; having made the effort to *understand* these needs they frequently aim too low in both appearance and function.

Where, then, does the individual user fit into the production and selling systems of industry and commerce? Practically nowhere. As a poor substitute for the consumer's one-time participation in the design and execution processes we have advertising and public relations. Although frequently maligned as disreputable pursuits, advertising and P.R. are, in the vast majority of cases, carried on by highly-trained, intelligent human beings, acting responsibly in the interests of their clients – the manufacturers. But they operate a one-way channel of communication; there is no answering voice from the consumers' end. And even if there were a come-back – a pause for discussion – the consumer in his present state of confusion would be soon out-gunned by the prodigious power which lies behind some of the techniques of persuasion in the armouries of advertising agencies. A well mounted public relations campaign is even more difficult to counter with innocent questions, because it works by remote control through the medium of editorial information in the Press and on television.

It is claimed that the user's voice is heard through the medium of market research. There is some truth in this. Manufacturers do genuinely want to know what fate lies in store for their next range of products. To find out they can employ a permanent market research staff of their own or hire it from one of the many specialized agencies, some of which belong to advertising companies. In rare cases the information they seek is elicited on a disinterested basis which allows expression to the potential user's real needs. More often, a market research survey is conducted with built-in preconceptions conditioned by the types of product the manufacturer wants to make. Here the potential user is presented with a choice of several designs and perhaps given a chance to try them out. His answers are eventually added up until a majority opinion shows the manufacturer which design to choose. From the user's viewpoint the inadequacy of the method is obvious – he or she may not really want any of the designs offered, or have the money to pay for them in the hazy future, and so potentially dishonest answers can be given simply to terminate a bothersome interview. All these dangers are well known to the market research organizations but they – like the consumer himself who becomes bemused with advertising – can do little to counteract the influence of the respondent who handles the truth rather loosely.

In the market place the user's contribution to the design process nowadays is almost wholly negative. He is left with finished designs only. And at that stage the only way of making a critical comment on a design is not to buy it. Should the manufacturer be bothered by this? He has only one sure way of telling whether a design is a success or not. And yet, the theory of establishing market response on the basis of sales results must be treated with reserve; it is in fact only valid when the price of the competitor's product is the same as the manufacturer's own. The attraction of selling goods by means of charging a little less than a competitor is likely to be one of the chief motivations of commerce for many years, especially in declining markets; the effective way in which it obscures any faithful expression of consumer demand must be recognized.

Having sketched in outline the commercial background to selling design, it is clear that we are left with one major uncertainty. Put in the form of a question it appears to be this: Does the individual consumer, when purchasing a new design, get what he wants? It may be said that he would not buy it if he were not satisfied, but in many cases the consumer is not able to abstain for he must meet a real need as nearly as he can. So he goes home either wholly or partially satisfied, and if it is the latter he must make his living habits – in fact his home – fit the new design as best he can.

We are of course concerned with *real* needs and not with

fashionable needs which, in industrial design for domestic use, reflect a taste for the modern, pseudo-modern, or period styles. People do buy according to one or other of the prevailing tastes. In nearly all groups of product they find they have to, or go without. And nothing in this essay is intended to disregard the element of fashion, for plenty of historical evidence can be submitted to show that a given age has its characteristic tastes or fashions. What is suggested is simply this: designers and manufacturers tend to rely too much on the superficial, trivial, and easily assimilated fashionable trends of the moment and too little on evidence of the user's real requirements. Such evidence would not only guide the functional aspect of designing, it would reliably inform the aesthetic aspect so that the product could make a new and vital contribution to style in its field.

Manufacturers and designers do not know with any reasonable accuracy what their public needs, because they do not know their public. Instead of working only on the basis of their own experience, and within the confines of the prevailing style, they should have at their command full reports of the way in which the consumer is *using* their last design or the designs of their competitors. What sort of people are their potential customers? How have they equipped their houses? If answers were found to these questions the designer working with the manufacturer and his team would have a real basis upon which to evolve the next product. It is quite fair, and necessary, for the designer to claim that he is a leader; that his work should create a demand. Yet it is seldom realized that the designer *cannot* be a step in front of his public if he and the manufacturer do not know the ground on which his public rests today.

Nowadays, with industry's predilection for grouping in order to economize in the production of a diminishing number of different designs, is it feasible to argue the case for closer contact between designer and user? Although physical contact with 10,000 or 20,000 potential customers is naturally out of the question, a great deal could be done to acquire up-to-date information about people's needs and preferences.

How could the research be carried out? In what way could

its results best give a lead to the designer? Some tentative suggestions can be made. To begin with, the central question to ask is: 'Why do you furnish your home in this way?' and not, with a sample product in each hand: 'Which design do you prefer?' We need to know – by observation as well as questioning – why people behave as they do, before asking them how they are likely to respond if a certain design came their way, at a time when they needed it and had the money to pay for it.

This information could be elicited by a survey, perhaps initially limited to certain areas of the country and, possibly, to certain income groups. The technique used by the market research organizations of taking a sample would be a necessary limitation, but it must be admitted that to get worth while results over sufficiently large areas and to keep the information up-to-date, the scheme would be costly.

If we suppose that such a proposal were adopted, say by several industries working together – or better still by several universities – then what type of information is needed? The designers would need to know how products made by their firms are used and misused. They would be able to discover, from reading the results of disinterested observation in different houses, where the gaps lay; where wholly unsuspected functions in family living suddenly achieved proportions significant enough to open up a new section of the market. The broad categories of heating, lighting, cooking, feeding, relaxing, sleeping, leisure, children, in-laws, and gardens show not only the scope of the inquiry but also its fascinating implications. A strange new world lies under our noses and none of us knows anything about it!

The danger of placing too much reliance on statistics should not, of course, be overlooked. The important role taken by accountants in modern business fastens what seems to be undue significance to figures. Armed with figures which indicate by percentages the public's opinion of certain ideas on design, the manufacturer can (and does) face his designer with what he believes to be an accurate statement of the customer's needs and tastes. The designer will often feel constrained to comply with the results of research. In doing so he may easily be persuaded to set aside his imagination which will become atrophied progressively as the initiative for new ideas passes from him to a market research organization which, again working by percentages, will be able to present a convincing picture of the product that people would like to buy in the future.

For these reasons the stress should be on the need for *disinterested* research carried out with the independence that universities or a philanthropic foundation are best able to furnish. The pattern of consumer needs and preferences would be built up progressively, year by year, recording not only the types of change, but also the pace of change. The manufacturer would then be able to direct the energies of his design team towards a creative revaluation of the product in terms of a revealed social pattern; not towards the supply of a series of artistic overcoats for a ready-made solution based on percentages.

Short of a regular supply of information on this scale, there is another – seemingly obvious – way in which a firm in the domestic appliance market can keep its designer in touch with his public. The importance of good after-sales service for powered domestic equipment is recognized by the firm which values its prestige. It would normally employ a team of trained service engineers to deal with day-to-day mishaps and also, in some cases, make regular visits to ensure that the equipment is functioning satisfactorily. These engineers have an almost wholly unrealized opportunity to collect information for the designer.

On their visits to houses – amounting to many thousands in the year – they could study the use and abuse of the equipment and hear constructive suggestions from customers to whom the proper functioning of the design and the way in which it fits in the home – both physically and aesthetically – are of personal importance. And yet very few manufacturers make significant use of this information; few, if any, encourage their engineers to do anything but servicing; probably only one or two arrange for the proper recording of the owners' suggestions and the engineers' observations so that they can be collated and fed back to the designers.

Leaving the producing side of design alone for a moment, let us see what the consumers can do for themselves. Can the organizations now set up to protect the interests of consumers be of any help? To begin with they are almost exclusively concerned with products on the market – not with products that *ought* to be on the market. Next, these products are tested, largely in the laboratory, to find out which – at a given price – can be expected to function satisfactorily and which are likely to fail, which are safe in use, which should give long service, and so on. Most important of all, the Consumers' Association publishes findings to its subscribers and, by journalistic reports, to the readers of most newspapers and, occasionally, to viewers of BBC television. These reports, especially when read in the original publications, provide an important point of contact between the consumer and the facts about products not otherwise available to him.

These published investigations can, of course, be useful to the designer too. C.A.'s magazine *Which?* has manufacturers among its subscribers and it may be supposed that any comment on a product – particularly an adverse comment – will be passed on pretty quickly to the design and production departments. Already there have been cases where criticism in the pages of *Which?* has resulted in the withdrawal of some products from the market, or radical modifications to others. This indirect service to the designer is salutary because, as we have seen, he has otherwise virtually no correspondence with the ultimate users of his product.

The mounting interest in consumer affairs at an organized, and often at an official, level is a phenomenon of the fifties. The first magazine to draw attention regularly to consumer problems was *Design*, the monthly journal of the CoID. Later, *Shopper's Guide* began publication, shortly to be followed by the wholly independent and vastly more successful *Which?* Now the Government has joined in officially, and, following the recommendation of its Committee on Consumer Protection, it has set up a new Consumer Council.

Although there is among the consumer protection bodies a desire to make industry aware of its shortcomings, the real problem facing the designer goes deeper. If he paid too much attention to complaints – some of them perhaps rather niggling – he would scarcely be able to design at all. Something much more positive is needed. If he is to be assailed by negative remarks about his work, then these should be balanced by unbiased inquiries into what people really do with his designs, when they use them and where they use them. It is only in this way that he can get a working basis for developing new products.

While there is, so far as this country is concerned, no research being done on the scale needed, isolated attempts have been made by disinterested bodies to determine localized living patterns. Professor Dennis Chapman carried out work of this nature among middle and working class families in Liverpool shortly after the last War. The Department of Scientific and Industrial Research – particularly the Building Research Station – has been investigating various aspects of human needs in the design of buildings for some ten years. The Station

has selected groups of persons who are at present living with the particular design feature about which information is desired. By choosing persons with this specific knowledge it is possible to obtain many details of behaviour and experience, as well as their likes and dislikes, and this information, when related to the appropriate technical and cost data, can provide the type of practical guidance which an architect or housing department requires.*

A far-sighted survey – though again chiefly of use to architects and builders – is *Homes for Today and Tomorrow*.† But its recommendations regarding storage, kitchens, and heating are, it is hoped, already essential reading in the relevant industries. The attitude adopted in the report could well provide a more detailed survey of user requirements with a promising beginning:

The starting point for thinking about houses and flats must be the activities that people want to undertake in them. This approach to the problem of design starts with a clear recognition of these various activities and their relative importance in social, family,

* Vere Hole: 'Houses and People', the *Guardian* 4 July 1962.
† Ministry of Housing and Local Government, H.M.S.O. 1961.

and individual lives, and goes on to assess the conditions necessary for their pursuit in terms of space, atmosphere, efficiency, comfort, furniture, and equipment.

Some other countries have tackled the problems of user needs – with an eye on educating the designer and manufacturer – in ways that would be beneficial if carried out in Britain. Chief among them are Holland and Sweden. In the former the Boucentrum, the Building Centre in Rotterdam, led and published research based on questionnaires which claimed to establish the essential working requirements of a house from the 'material, moral, cultural, and social points of view'. Dutch firms followed up by mass-producing equipment in accordance with the recommendations. In Sweden industry has similarly followed the lead given by disinterested surveys, such as those produced by that country's Institute for Consumer Research and by its Society of Industrial Design. In Britain we have the newly created Research Institute for Consumer Affairs, which is beginning to publish some useful information.

More public agitation to produce basic, required information of this type is plainly needed. For far too long British consumers have been left to flounder in a pile of communications from industry each one having reached them on a one-way ticket at velocities that vary according to the type of publicity machine employed. And yet industry would gain as much as the user if it knew more precisely for whom it was catering. With information on use its output would be better designed for specific markets and so stay in production for relatively longer periods – a feature that would do much to absolve firms from the annual rat-race to create gimmicky styles in order to gain a temporary advantage over their competitors. The 'Radio Show' is a good example of this sort of waste; so is the 'Furniture Show': both of them annual events with national coverage in the Press and on television.

It is significant that designers who work in accordance with the requirements of specific users are to be found in the relatively remote fields of control equipment for heavy mechanical plant and electronic equipment. Here the production runs tend to be short, with a consequently greater opportunity to vary designs. For example, in the design of crane cabs the laboratory of the British Iron and Steel Research Association has carried out experiments to determine the optimum visibility and comfort for the operator. The result yields the twin rewards of greater efficiency and increased safety: factors worth spending money on when an alternative *laissez-faire* attitude should so obviously be avoided.

The housewife leaning over the sink with her back near breaking point may well claim that the necessity to improve her lot is equally obvious. Her efficiency could undoubtedly be improved if the sink were suited to her height and arm reach; her health, in the long run, may well be impaired because these obvious physical factors have been neglected. Manufacturers of this and other kitchen equipment have little published information to guide them. It is perhaps too much to ask them to translate the results of comparable research carried out in Sweden, and so we are left with the entirely arbitrary British Standard working top height: arrived at more by accident than design, and certainly not based on research.

British research *is* done in this anthropometrical field, but only for relatively critical needs, ranging from fighter pilots to school children. The Air Force set up a laboratory in the early years of the War to determine the best forms of aircraft seating, the optimum accessibility of controls and the most convenient types and sizes of clothing. Work on these problems is still being done at Farnborough. For school children several attempts have been made to establish the best sizes and shapes for desks and chairs for different ages; the most notable was conducted at Birmingham University and its findings have been used as the basis for the British Standard sizes. But, as most people know, these standards are voluntary and both manufacturers and local education authorities can depart from them if they wish. While a lead has been given (notably by the Ministry of Education's architect's department in the equipping of experimental schools) the problem has not yet been faced by those most responsible for its solution. State schools may be more advanced than private schools – though certain notable exceptions exist among the latter (especially when they belong to the so-called 'progressive' category) – but it is not hard to find a school equipped with furniture all of exactly the same size for use by children aged between eleven and seventeen years.

If that is one of the more critical cases deserving attention what, we may ask, is being done to make the multifarious activities of adults more convenient? Take the secretary for example. Here is a person whose duties are being performed by hundreds of thousands of girls throughout the country. We know (from reliable statistics) that forty per cent of women wearing heels of one and a half inches or less will be uncomfortable on a chair seventeen inches high. But from most dealers we are still likely to be offered British made chairs that cannot be screwed down below seventeen inches.

This is not the place to go into the anatomical reasons why, because of these chairs, the majority of secretaries and typists are to a greater or lesser extent uncomfortably seated. They are a case deserving not so much research as recognition; in seating of this kind the problem is relatively obvious and it is merely ignorance which prevents a solution to suit every girl.

In situations where people are constantly changing their positions to perform different tasks there is less need for this earnest research. It is very easy to take up the cudgels blindly and wield them against the seeming indifference of manufacturers. But having said that, it should be stressed that there are still many acres of virgin territory which qualify for an urgent inquiry. With the number of deaths on the road reaching something like 6,000 a year, we may wonder how much might be gained if our motor manufacturers and their design teams recognized that the driver's sitting position had something to do with safety on the roads. British research is slender and uncoordinated. And yet, in a trial investigation carried out by *Design* magazine, it was proved beyond doubt that better seating positions, better visibility, and better systems of manual control would tend to reduce the likelihood of accidents.

What must be realized is the fact that for some types of consumer research the old head-counting methods are not enough.

The manipulation of anthropometrical data requires skill, but that skill is available. A new branch of science – an amalgam of different disciplines – is slowly gaining ground, in response first to the critical needs of the Services. It is known as 'ergonomics' and it brings together experimental physiologists and psychologists. Ergonomics, a term derived from the Greek words for measuring the laws of work, means to us the study of man in his working environment. Somewhat easier on the tongue, but unfortunately ambiguous, is the American term 'human engineering', used to describe the same thing.

Man, in certain circumstances, presents a problem more complex than has hitherto been realized. Specialists must be brought in to investigate and so interpret his needs to the designer. We should not be put off by the intrusion of such words as psychology here; this is not psychiatry and the Freudian couch, but applied experimental psychology. Its vocabulary is normal, its results are not abstruse, and as such they are immediately intelligible to the designer.

The central problem is the need for the designer to appreciate his public. He cannot obtain this knowledge by relying on the standard market research techniques. It is simply no good asking people what they would like to have in their homes when they, at the moment when the interviewer catches them, have no intention of making a real decision based on what they need and can afford. It is for the manufacturer to ensure that his designer's knowledge is based on a more circumspect inquiry; possibly one which continues for a long period, needs to be most carefully planned and is not likely to be cheap. But from what has already been brought to light from sporadic studies in this country and abroad, there can be no doubt that anything less fundamental is merely toying with the problem.

Each manufacturer and designer should select the type of research he needs and can afford. The consumer organizations could help in this if the wider – more preventative rather than curative – aspects of their work were recognized. After all, this plea has an essentially common-sense origin. Once the maker of a thing knew the man for whom he made it; now, his successor, in the era of quantity production, cannot meet his potential customers. The more this gap is recognized the narrower it will get.

'Consumption is the sole end and purpose of production ...' said Adam Smith, and few manufacturers today would not agree with him. However, the last half of his sentence is not so palatable '... and the interest of the producer ought to be attended to only so far as it may be necessary for promoting that of the consumer'. Such single-mindedness sounds naïve today, and yet the truth shines out of it. It is not research surveys alone – however well conceived – that will give the consumer a sporting chance to discriminate profitably among manufactured articles. He must recognize that there are powerful pressure groups in industry and commerce and, surprisingly within himself and within other consumers, that fight hard for interests expensively invested in the *status quo*.

Take the consumer first: he is pathetically reliant on traditional ways of thinking and behaving; he is nervous of being called *avant garde* (confused political overtones are heard); he hates experiment; he blindly follows fashions (provided his friends keep abreast of him). Faced with this pig-headed fellow being – variously called consumer, man-in-the-street or Mrs Housewife – can we wonder that commerce takes a short cut to quick returns and manipulates him into submission, or at least as far as the first down-payment? And when he does re-assert his individuality in order to write to the newspapers about how ill he is used at home (by his inanimate possessions) how soon will he succumb again, lighting the fire with the latest issue of *Which?* and go whoring after the promise of the bigger, brighter, better something or other he wants but does not need?

Enough has probably been said about the myopia of industry for us to cut short its consideration here. Lack of far-sightedness is one trait; downright cynicism is another – to the question 'What do you make?' the manufacturer replied 'Oh, about £30,000 a year.' Then there are the industrial groupings which carve out territories for themselves to cut down 'wasteful' competition and so effectively limit the consumer's choice.

Enough has probably not been said about commerce, particularly about the retailer, who holds his whip-hand somewhere between the two protagonists, flaying to right and left with enviable ambidexterity. He may refuse to stock a brilliantly conceived design offered to him on the one side, but he will seldom fail to make a sale of its inferior predecessor to some bemused but hungry consumer on the other. As a communication vehicle the retailer is perversely clogged; from the remark that 'No one has complained before, Sir', he will turn to the next incensed customer and say exactly the same thing.

Though few retailers actually do behave in the manner suggested by this grossly exaggerated portrait, they do on many, many occasions fail to take advantage creatively of their position as a two-way traffic system for producer and user information. All too often the road is up on one lane – (Bargain sales) – or there is a series of head-on collisions between guarantees signed in 1964 and the Sale of Goods Act 1893 – with the retailer standing to one side like a sleepy traffic cop.

Before any policy to conduct thorough inquiries into market needs is embarked upon, the realistic manufacturer will want to be assured that the potential consumer of its fruits will at least get to hear about them. To assist him he can call on the other already established aids to commerce – advertising and public relations. They would refurbish his public image with some conviction if they could base it on such a new policy. The opportunity would be unique. 'Here, at last', they would say, 'is a range of designs specifically suited to YOUR needs'; and at last they would be right.

How would the user react? He is still an individual, and he will instinctively realize that he is being offered a product from a mass-producing system and that others are being offered it too. The advertisement can fairly claim – if the manufacturer has done his homework properly – that this product is the nearest possible approximation to the user's real needs. And for the majority that should be convincing.

But how much more convincing would it be if the whole conception of a market inquiry had been on a grander scale? Here would be not one manufacturer, but two dozen manufacturers, each in a separate industry, but each making a product for use in the home. The prospect becomes attractive to both main parties: the manufacturers share the costs of research and promotion; the user finds that for the very first time in the twentieth century he and his family have been thought of systematically as a living, evolving organism – and supplied accordingly. For the amount of convenience and aesthetic pleasure he will derive from an integrated home he may well feel that the need to refurnish drastically is more important than a new car and a holiday. And even if he did not step out so boldly, the hire purchase terms that would be offered by a large consortium of firms could be made exceedingly attractive to him.

System is, of course, a key word in a new context. It precludes piecemeal thinking and offers both designers and users an integrated complex of functions, needs, and preferences. It prevents wasteful overlap; say in the provision of storage space, methods of lighting, or the powered element in powered appliances, to name only a few examples. And when some technically original design is brought on to the market later the maker will know what type of shape and dimensions to adopt to ensure that it precisely replaces its predecessor in the domestic system.

This is not so Wellsian as it seems. To remain profitable more and more firms are having to devote time and money to market planning. It is but a short step to persuade them that the information they should plan with is that which reflects real needs and not merely the sales results of their competitor's current models. Or is it?

One new aspect of the current uncoordinated complex of domestic design is of striking importance. The consumer is not only becoming enlightened about what to buy and what not to buy, he is becoming articulate as well. This is a development that will help designers, help manufacturers, and indeed help whole industries – but only if they step in quickly and organize the discussion. This, after all, is their privilege. The consumer who says 'I know what I like' can be the most inaccurate barometer of all. He cannot know what he likes until the

195

manufacturer has made it – and if he does not like it then it will be just too bad for both of them.

*

SOURCES OF HELP

Council of Industrial Design: The Education Officer organizes a panel of lecturers, mainly professional people, who are expert in their own subjects which include design in the home, colour and pattern, and domestic products generally. If aids to the teaching of design are needed, also get in touch with the Education Officer who in addition arranges group visits to the Design Centre. Lantern slides may be obtained from the Council's photographic library on payment of a small hiring charge. Council of Industrial Design, The Design Centre, 28 Haymarket, London SW1.

Design and Industries Association: This is an unofficial group of enthusiasts among whom are teachers, architects, designers, manufacturers, and retailers. The DIA has a London headquarters and 11 regional branches in Birmingham, Bristol, Leicester, Leeds, Manchester, North East, North Staffordshire, Nottingham, Oxford, Sheffield, and Scotland. The current membership is 1,400 and is growing daily. Its functions are interdisciplinary meetings in London and elsewhere to discuss a very wide variety of design topics. There are special arrangements for including whole schools, both staff and students, in the membership. Full details from the General Secretary, Design and Industries Association, 13 Suffolk Street, London SW1.

BOOKS

P. REYNER BANHAM, *Theory and Design in the First Machine Age* (Architectural Press, 1960)

HENRY DREYFUSS, *Designing for People* (Simon and Schuster, New York, 1955)

MICHAEL FARR, *Design in British Industry – a Mid-Century Survey* (Cambridge University Press, 1955)

SIEGFRIED GIEDION, *Mechanization takes Command* (Oxford University Press, New York, 1948)

ELIZABETH GUNDREY, *Your Money's Worth – a Handbook for Consumers* (Penguin, 1962)

GEORGE NELSON, *Problems of Design* (Whitney Publications, New York, 1957)

NIKOLAUS PEVSNER, *Pioneers of Modern Design* (Pelican, 1960)

MAGAZINE

Design, magazine of the Council of Industrial Design, monthly, 3s. 6d.

Notes on Contributors

PHILIP ABRAMS is a Fellow of Peterhouse, Cambridge, and Assistant Lecturer in Sociology: started out as a historian, then went to the London School of Economics as a sociologist and lectured on the mass media and popular culture. Mainly interested now in fashion, popular music, and politics: almost a television addict. His wife, Sonia Abrams, is Secretary of the Advisory Centre for Education. They have one son, Dominic, aged four, who refuses to share his father's low interests.

MICHAEL FARR was at Wycliffe College and Downing College, Cambridge, where he read English. After four years as a pilot in the R.A.F. he was successively News Editor of the *Architects' Journal*, Editor of *Design*, and Chief Information Officer to the Council of Industrial Design. In 1962 he started his own design management consultancy – Michael Farr (Design Integration) Ltd. He is also General Secretary, Design and Industries Association. His *Design in British Industry* (CUP) is the result of two years' research.

DAVID HOLBROOK is thirty-nine and a Fellow of King's College, Cambridge. He read English at Downing College. He has worked in adult education, in secondary modern schools, and journalism. Publications include two books of poetry, short stories, a book on *Children's Games*, one on modern poetry (*Llareggub Revisited*) and one on teaching English (*English for Maturity*). He has also written a number of books for schools; others, and a novel, *Flesh Wounds*, are in preparation.

DONALD J. HUGHES, aged forty-nine, was educated at Brighton, Hove, and Sussex G.S., where music – not being on the curriculum – became his absorbing interest. Later he took both a B.Sc. in Economics and a Doctorate in Music. After the Army he became Music Adviser in Middlesex and is now Lecturer in Music at Hendon Technical College. He is chairman of several Committees on music, and his publications include *Let's Have Some Music*. He believes that far too many musicians are interested only in music and not in people.

ALBERT HUNT, thirty-four, was educated at Accrington G.S., and Balliol, where he read Modern Languages. After teaching in a Norfolk grammar school he became Tutor in Adult Education in Shropshire, where he lectures on literature, theatre, and the mass media. He has written a pamphlet for the British Film Institute and essays on film and theatre for *New Left Review*, *New University*, *Encore*, and *Peace News*. He is a member of the BFI Lecture Panel.

GRAHAM MARTIN was born in Glasgow in 1927. Went to school at Glasgow High School, and Glenalmond, Perthshire. Took B.Sc., at St Andrews University, and after a year in USA on an exchange scholarship, and a year teaching science, read English at Jesus College, Oxford, and subsequently did research at Merton College. First university job at Leeds University, and then to Bedford College, London, where now a lecturer. Published essay on Yeats in *The Modern Age* (Pelican Guide to English Literature), and occasional reviews in *New Statesman* and *New Left Review*.

FRANK WHITEHEAD was until lately a lecturer in English at the University of London Institute of Education, and is now senior lecturer in English and Education at the University of Sheffield Institute of Education. He wrote the essay on George Crabbe in Volume 5 of the *Pelican Guide to English Literature*, and has also edited a volume of selections from Crabbe's poetry.

Some other Pelican books are described
on the following pages

Personal Values in the Modern World

M. V. C. Jeffreys

The future of our civilization depends on the
extent to which we can rescue and promote personal
values. The Professor of Education at Birmingham
University discusses in this book the need for the
rediscovery of a coherent view of life, the achievement
of intelligent and effective communication between
people and groups of people, and the encouragement
of voluntary action both alongside and within
public administration. The undermining of individual
responsibility and mutual human respect by the
impersonal mass-production of a 'faceless' culture
is essentially an educational problem, and the
main aspects of education are therefore
discussed at some length.

The Necessity of Art
A Marxist Approach

Ernst Fischer

On the first appearance in English of what is
probably one of the most influential books on art to
be published since the war, Kenneth Tynan wrote:

'In this challenging new Pelican Ernst Fischer, the
Austrian poet and critic, surveys the whole history
of artistic achievement through Marxist eyes.

People have always needed art: but why have they
needed it? And what shaped the forms whereby
they satisfied their need? Fischer's answers to these
questions should be as voraciously studied and
debated here as they have been on the Continent.

The book abounds in signs that Fischer is an empirical
rather than a doctrinaire Marxist; you never feel
he is tailoring his reactions to fit a thesis. "A new
art," he says, "does not come out of doctrines but
out of works. Aristotle did not precede . . . Homer,
Hesiod, Aeschylus and Sophocles; he derived his
aesthetic theories from them."

Marxism has long needed an Aristotle; and in
Ernst Fischer I suspect it has found its man.'

This book was first published in East Germany
in 1959.

The Contemporary Cinema

Penelope Houston

Of the total history of the cinema one quarter
belongs to the years since the war. *The Contemporary
Cinema* thus ranges from neo-realism to the new
wave, from *On the Town* to five years of
South Pacific, from the Gainsborough Lady to
This Sporting Life; and the directors include not
only Antonioni, Truffaut, and Anderson, but also
Renoir, Buñuel, and de Sica; not only Ford,
Hitchcock, and Hawks, but also Kubrick, Ray, and
Cassavetes.

In a sustained, imaginative survey of the whole
post-war scene, Penelope Houston, the Editor of
Sight and Sound, shows how the cinema has
adjusted itself to meet a new audience which
approaches films more critically than before, but in
doing so encourages new talent. At the same time
she makes clear the industrial problems (in particular,
the fight to co-exist with TV) which are inseparable
from the business of film-making. The book is
illustrated with over 30 plates, and a check-list of
films provides a guide to more than one
hundred directors.

'It does extremely well what it is meant to do,
provide a quick glimpse of what has happened
globally to films since the last, or Second, World War
... I cannot think of a better short survey of
world cinema at present' – Andrew Sinclair
in the *Spectator*

'An extremely readable and much-needed assessment
of films and their makers since the war' – Eric
Shorter in the *Daily Telegraph*

The Comprehensive School

Robin Pedley

Nearly everyone interested in education today
wants to abolish the 11 + examination, but few
people are clear what the alternatives are.

The best alternative is some form of comprehensive
school and in this new appraisal the Director of
the Exeter University Institute of Education gives a
clear and critical picture of the comprehensive school
as it exists in England and Wales today. Dr Pedley
first describes just what the 11 + is and does. Then,
after dispelling the bogey that comprehensive
schools need at least two thousand pupils in order to
function, he goes on to demonstrate, by statistics,
that those in existence are already rivalling the
tripartite system in academic achievements. Finally,
and most important, he argues that a good
comprehensive school can both focus and mirror a
community as can no other school.

Of all our educational establishments the
comprehensive school is the least understood.
This book, which contains a glossary of educational
terms and a list of comprehensive schools, offers
to interested readers – especially parents –
all the facts.

Educating the Intelligent

Michael Hutchinson and
Christopher Young

If the Battle of Waterloo was won on the
playing-fields of Eton, it is equally true that Britain's
destiny is today being hammered out in the classrooms
of secondary schools all over the country. Recent
controversies have raised many questions about the
direction which is being taken by secondary
education. Is it correctly orientated for the needs of
modern society or does it tend to 'level downwards'?
Should more encouragement be given to pupils
who are above the average intelligence? Ought we
deliberately to train an élite?

The two authors of this constructive and absorbing
book have had many years' experience as teachers.
After exposing some of the serious inadequacies
of the present curriculum in secondary schools,
they go on to analyse the basic educational needs
of the intelligent child. They then outline an
alternative curriculum which would both meet these
needs and be practicable within the average
secondary school. In addition, they discuss fully the
sixth-form syllabus, the examination system,
university selection, and the choice, training,
and remuneration of teachers.

Soviet Education

Nigel Grant

Interest in Soviet education has intensified recently,
due to an increasing public awareness of educational
problems in general. There has, however, so far
been a lack of a short, up-to-date, comprehensive
account of the Russian educational system.

In this study Nigel Grant not only describes the
different types of schools and colleges in the
U.S.S.R., and the work they do, but also examines
the educational system as a whole against its
geographical, historical, social, and political
background. As well as giving a very vivid impression
of life in Soviet schools, he provides much
fascinating material for comparison with our own
educational theories and problems.

The author is a lecturer on educational theory
at Jordanhill College of Education in Scotland.

*For a complete list of books available please write to
Penguin Books whose address can be found on the back
of the title page*

DATE DUE